The Russian Experience
Ideas in History

The Russian Experience

Ideas in History

Edited by

N. Maslova and T. Pleshakova

Nova Science Publishers, Inc.

Art Director: Christopher Concannon
Graphics: Elenor Kallberg and Maria Ester Hawrys
Manuscript Coordinator: Roseann Pena
Book Production: Tammy Sauter, Benjamin Fung
and Michelle Lalo
Circulation: Irene Kwartiroff and Annette Hellinger

*Library of Congress Cataloging–in–Publication Data
available upon request*

ISBN 1-56072-211-8

© *1995 Nova Science Publishers, Inc.*
6080 Jericho Turnpike, Suite 207
Commack, New York 11725
Tele. 516-499-3103 Fax 516-499-3146
E Mail Novasci1@aol.com

Printed in the United States of America

CONTENTS

PREFACE

This collection brings together some of the prominent thinkers of the Russian experience. It is an experience based on centuries of great achievements in art, music, literature, dance and philosophy as well as in science, commerce and religion. Sad to say, its treasures have remained and will probably will continue to remain hidden from anyone without a solid knowledge of the Russian language.

In this book, we delve into consciousness and civilization, the historical process, social history, art, language and the anti-utopia. Many of the thoughts expressed in the works presented here were forerunners of much better known Western thinkers. Hidden by the beauty of the Russian language is a colossal depth of Russian experience and much to be learned and appreciated. We hope the readers of this small book find a few morsels to ponder and to perhaps lead them to further explorations in whichever direction their curiosity goes.

Frank Columbus
Publisher

CONSCIOUSNESS AND CIVILISATION

Merab Mamardashvili[*]

The theme of this title is wide-ranging and evokes a great many associations. I see it though as something specific and in the context of the present-day situation which worries me and in which I distinguish certain features that make me think of a structure which may prove irreversible and which therefore appalls me and elicits a desire to reason it out and see if there is a general law underlying it I all. It is therefore with a mixed feeling of horror and curious amazement that I want to put forward certain arguments on this score.

To set the tone of the argument, I would like to describe its hub as follows. I have a feeling that of the great number of cataclysms for which the 20th century is notorious, and which threaten us now, the principal one, and the one most often concealed from view, is the I anthropological disaster. It is not expressed in such breath-taking I events as an asteroid hitting the earth, as depletion of the earth's natural resources or excessive population growth, or even as an ecological or nuclear tragedy. I refer to an event which involves man himself, and which is connected with civilisation in the sense that ii something vitally important may irreversibly break down in him because of the destruction or simply the absence of civilised foundation of the process of life.

Civilisation is like a very fragile flower or structure, and it has become quite clear in the 20th century that this flower or edifice, with cracks all over it, is threatened with destruction. This destruction of the foundations of civilisation is doing something to the human element, to the human material of life, being expressed in an anthropological cataclysm which is probably the prototype of all I the other possible catastrophes. It can occur, and partially does occur, due to the

[*] M. **Mamardashvili**, D. Sc. (Philos.), Author of books *Forms and Content of Thinking, The Classical and Non-Classical Ideal of Rationality* and of articles on the methodology of philosophical analysis and problems of consciousness.

violation of ontological laws determining the framework of human consciousness underlying human civilisation.

As I read about more than a dozen global catastrophes imagined by Isaac Asimov and among them the earth's possible encounter with a microcosmic black hole, I am inclined to believe that such a hole already exists in an everyday sense familiar to us all, that we Earthmen fairly often take a dip in it, since everything that passes beyond the screen and falls into this hole immediately disappears and becomes inaccessible, the two sides of the contact being annihilated, as must be the case in contacts with black holes. There apparently exists a certain unified fundamental structure of consciousness; apparently this consciousness exists objectively and is rooted in the ontology of the Universe, so that the heterogeneous, externally unconnected with each other and logically remote from each other, microscopic, macroscopic, and macrocosmic phenomena observed by the philosopher are viewed by him as extensive analogies. In a sense, these phenomena can be regarded as metaphors of the properties of consciousness objectively incorporated in the structure of the cosmos (to the extent to which it can be observed by man, and to which man can realise himself in it).

I shall use these metaphors of inaccessibility, disappearance, and behind-the-screen conflict to explain my chain of reasoning. But first let me quote a poem by Gottfried Benn. The depth of this poet's insights is connected with the reality of the experience, a personal experience from within, of living under the conditions of a definite system, of experience which an external, distant observer cannot have. Now, this poem, called (for a very good reason) "The Whole", describes the fate of this inner knowledge and of its carrier, man.

> Some were in commotion, others in tears, in some hours, there
> was a radiance, and more, in these years, there was the heart, in
> those were storms—whose storms—who?

> Never in happiness, seldom accompanied, mostly concealed, for
> it happened in the depth, and all the streams ran on, growing,
> and all things external got close to the inside.

> One looked at you hard, another looked at you milder, one saw
> things structured, another, destroyed, but what they saw were
> half-pictures, for the whole belongs only to you.

> At the beginning it was clearer what you wanted and aimed at
> and was near believing, but when you saw what you had to,
> what looked down on the whole turning to stone,

it was not glamour and not fire in which your look, the last one, was lost: A naked head, in blood, a monster, on whose eyelash there hung a tear.

The concluding image of this poem is just as clear as its inner linkages, all of them homing on "the whole", or the *sensation* of the whole experienced by the poet, a special mood of elation and possession of the *essence* of the world mystery—something that I call inner experience of strange systems inaccessible to a distant external observer, experience in which (and that is the whole point) man the carrier is inaccessible to himself. For the fact is that, in the very nature of things, a man is not all in man, and he moves towards himself from a great distance. And never reaches himself, in this case. These linkages of the poem will figure, in one form or another, in the exposition below.

THE THREE K'S PRINCIPLE

The whole of the argument below will be focussed on a definite principle permitting, on the one hand, to characterise situations which I shall call describable or normal (in these situations there is no "mystique of the whole", which we find in the poem, although they are wholes), and on the other, situations which I shall call indescribable or involving strangeness. These two types of situations are related, or mutually reflexive in a mirror-like fashion, since, among other reasons, everything that happens in them can be expressed in one and the same language, i.e. in the same referential nominations and sign sense equivalents (designations), and in their syntax. There is "inner knowledge" in both cases here. In the second case, though, it actually degenerates into a system of self imitations. Although the language remains the same, it is dead ("dead words smell bad", as poet Gumilyov said).

Indescribable situations, or situations that defy description, can also be called situations of fundamental indeterminateness. When this property is separated off and realised in pure form, the situations in question are precisely the kind of "black holes" in which whole peoples and vast human spaces can fall.

I shall call the principle which orders these two types of situations the Three K's Principle—the principle of Cartesius (Descartes),** Kant and Kafka. The formulation of the principle I offer is as follows. The first K (Descartes): a certain elementary and immediately obvious "I am" actually takes place in the world. This "I am" is an irreplaceable and unique realisation of man in the thought he implements (separately from existence, a thought that is further indi-

---

** The name begins with K in the Russian transcription—Ed.

visible, unrepresentable and inexpressible in language, or ideally). This *cogito,* doubting everything else, does not merely act as the all-pervading realisation of the dependence of all events taking place in the world (in knowledge, too) on man's own actions but is also a point of absolute truth and obviousness for any knowledge formulated by thought. In its turn, the world is such that this nonverbal, actually functioning being or capability, the living existence of yourself (irreplaceable and unique) in thought and its consequences is an *event* realised at a point according to the event's own laws of possibility, and minimally sufficient for the world to be an entire whole. In other words, the being *capable* of saying "I think, I exist, I can" (even, minimally, a single being) is precisely the possibility and condition of the world—a world which it can understand, in which it can humanly act, in which it can be responsible for something and know something with good reason. For the world to exist, it is enough, let me repeat, that this should happen to one single being at any place and at any time. If things were different in this world, if there were no "tuning" of the world—the famous Cartesian connection and unity of all things *(mathesis universalis)*—then nothing like that would happen. But it did happen, it has been stated in an act of thought, in a state-event. The world has thus been *created* (in the sense of the law of formation). The rest is up to you. For the world that is created is such that you *can* be capable of, whatever the visible counter-necessities of nature, spontaneous-elemental compelling forces and circumstances.

It is easy to recognise in these formulas the *cogito ergo sum* principle, to which I have given a form that better suits its real content. If this first principle, i.e. *cogito* in the sense of "I can", is not realised, or if " I think" is not established each time anew by the available vital force of the nonverbal existences in the moment of and within consciousness (if the field of consciousness is destroyed, for instance), everything is inevitably filled with ready-made nihilism, which can be succinctly described as the "only not-I can" principle (i.e. everyone and everything else can—other men, God, circumstances, natural necessities, etc.). In other words, this involves the assumption of a spontaneously active mechanism working instead of me (whether it be the "mechanism" of happiness, social and moral well-being, Supreme Providence, etc.). The *cogito* principle asserts: *only with, on and through me,* given my own labour and spiritual effort aimed at my liberation and development; which is, of course, the most difficult thing on earth. But that is the only way in which the soul can receive and germinate the "highest" seed, that is to say, to rise above itself and the circumstances, as a result of which all that takes place around one proves to be non-irreversible, non-final, not given entirely and fully by the causal chain of the flow of natural necessity. In other words, it is not humanly hopeless. In this eternally forming world, there is always room for me and my action, if I am ready to begin everything anew, to begin with myself, the one that has become.

The second K (Kant): the structure of the world, which incorporates man's life, contains special necessarily postulated and *active* hypothetical, intelligible objects or dimensions which are at the same time immediately, experimentally stable, if further indivisible, *images* of wholes, plans or designs for development, as it were. They carry in themselves a certain synthetic fact happening for the first time, and serve as "thing metaphors" for the survey ability of the entire whole, of its style and tone of existence; they are, as it were, a special stable matter of the inner form of consciousness ("inner knowledge") and orientation of living beings in the system. The strength of this principle lies in the fact that it points to the *conditions* of a finite being reasonably performing empirical acts of knowledge, moral action, assessment, sense of gratification during the search, etc. Otherwise nothing would have any meaning, with infinity lying ahead (and behind). In other words, that means that, complementary to an "I" contained in the field of rational apperception, conditions are realised in the world under which these acts are meaningful at all (with meaning being always discrete and localised). So it is assumed that the world could be of a kind in which these acts would be meaningless. The realisation of moral actions, evaluation, and searching desire has meaning only for a finite being. For an infinite, wholly existent and omnipotent being, the questions of their meaningfulness do not even arise and are thus solved. For a finite being, it is all conditional: everything depends on whether or not a primary synthesis, a really performed synthetic fact, occurred. If it did occur, and was defined, it is assumed that its repeated realisations are possible everywhere and at all times through the interaction of things with regard to everything that forms part of the delimitated domain and can be a real, solvable problem, everything that can be a real search. And that means that it is not always and not everywhere that we can speak of good and bad, beautiful and ugly, true and false, even in the presence of natural referents and corresponding words. Thus if an animal has eaten another animal, or prevailed over its brother in the same species by brute force, we cannot say with absolute certainty whether that is good or evil, just or unjust. This holds true of ritual human sacrifice. All this can be a pre-minimal world, or simply another world which makes the very formulation of such questions meaningless. The modern man usually speaks in terms of evaluations. We must not forget, though, that the conditions are here assumed to have been carried out which in general make our claim to acts of cognition, moral evaluation, etc. meaningful. The second K principle therefore asserts: some thing is meaningful since there are special "mentally perceived objects" ("intelligible characters", in Kant's terminology) or immobile all-pervading linkages (from the primary fact of synthesis which is not arbitrarily implemented by ourselves and is therefore further indivisible) in the structure of the world itself, linkages which guarantee this right and this meaningfulness. These worlds are naturally in the plural.

It is easy to see that this principle develops the Cartesian premise of the all-pervading connectedness and unity of things, a further linking-up of this premise to the problem of the duration and unity of *cogito*.

Finally, the third K (Kafka): given the same external signs and referential nominations and observability of their natural referents, all that is specified by the two above principles and that animates these signs—observability, etc.—are absent and not implemented here. This is the degenerated or regressive instance of the action of the general K-principle, for we have here zombi situations that are quite humanlike but in actual fact belong to a world different from man's, imitating what is actually dead. Their product is not *Homo sapiens,* i.e. man who *knows* good and evil, but "strange man", "indescribable man" (in the sense of the possibility to ascribe to him some qualities whose verbal designations already exist in language), the phantom *Homo specularis*—the real carrier of nihilism.

In terms of the general meaning of the three K's principle, the whole problem of human being consists in the fact that something has to be *turned,* again and again, into a situation amenable to a meaningful assessment and solution in the existential terms of ethics and personal dignity; that is to say, into a situation of freedom, or rejection of freedom as one of its own possibilities. In other words, morality is not the triumph of a definite system of morality (e.g. "good society", "an excellent institution", "an ideal person") compared to something opposite but the creation and ability for reproduction of a situation amenable to a meaningful application to it of the terms of morality and attainment by the latter (and only by them) of the uniqueness and completeness of its description. In short, given an operative and living force of distinguishing between good and evil, the terms of morality will pass from the pre-historical and pre-value-oriented world into a historical and value-oriented one.

But it also means that there exist certain first acts, or acts of world containment (absolutes) pertaining to the Kantian intelligibilities and Cartesian *cogito ergo sum.* It is through these that mall, at an advanced stage, actually contains, or can contain, the world and man himself as part of the world reproduced by it (which is the absolute good) as the subject of human demands, expectations, living perception, moral and cognitive criteria of a meaningful search. For instance, the artist's eye is the first act of containment and of testing nature as a landscape (outside this irreversible state nature cannot by itself be a source of appropriate human feelings). Or, say, a certain socio-religious articulation (from *religio* "link", specified, e.g. by the totem) is a vessel for a certain ensemble of men *as society.* Outside this link the latter is simply an unexplained interlacing of certain forces, instincts, appetites, and natural passions. In other words, the state or act of first containment cannot contradict itself, just as reason cannot contradict itself. The self-destruction of this act (i.e. the destruction of the conditions for the wholes and self-harmonisations indicated above) is evil, absolute evil; if the latter cannot be distinguished, the possibility itself and the fullness of *relative* evaluations, comparisons and identifications, do not exist.

In real terms, that means the following: a philosophical problem connected with consciousness and its ontology is reducible then to the fact that no natural referential description (from the outside) of acts of injustice, violence, etc., analytically contains, in meanings and referents/objects, any causes for our feelings of indignation, anger, of value-oriented experiences in general, in the absence of a synthetic addition of actual ("practical") implementation or givenness of a reasonable state, of that which Kant called the "facts of reason". These are not reasonable knowledge of concrete facts, of their reflection, so to speak, but reason itself as realised consciousness which cannot be assumed beforehand, introduced as an assumption, replaced by the "powerful mind", etc. Consciousness can only either be or not be. If such a fact exists, it is omnipresent and omnitemporal in the field of the possibilities of language and history it opens up (or in the space-time of primary semioticisation). For example, we cannot say that a certain tribe in Africa lives immorally, or that something moral happens in England and something immoral in Russia, without realising exactly this latent premise which I have expressed in the form of the first and the second formulas of the K-principle. For the natural referents and meanings of the description of that which takes place do not contain anything, analytically; they do not contain the states of space-time for thought and the things of thought, which alone make a phenomenon a connected event. And that is only probable, not logically immanent. But if the acts of first containment do *exist* and have been performed, and if we are part of their continuity, if we are incorporated in the continuity, we can state something meaningfully, expecting and achieving a completeness and uniqueness of description.

SITUATIONS OF INDETERMINACY

In third-K situations, ordinarily called absurd situations, and externally described by the same referential or sign nominations (as the first type of situations—Ed.), there are no acts of first world containment, or else they are reduced; although the language which carries in itself intentions and logical possibilities continues to speak in them in the same way as it always does. In other words, such situations differ in kind from their own language, and do not have human commensurability (it is as if an underdeveloped body of one nature expressed itself and gave an account of itself in head articulated in quite a different nature). They resemble a nightmare in which any attempt to think and to understand oneself, any search for the truth would end in a search for the toilet. The Kafkian man uses language and follows the pathos of his searching intentions in states that are definitely remote from the performance of the (logically primary) acts of

first containment different in nature from the manifestation of man's characteristic features. The latter is for him a purely mechanical way out of the situation, its
automatic solution, a choice between finding and not finding. That is why this
indescribably strange person is not tragic but absurd and ridiculous, especially in
his quasi-exalted aspirations. That is the comedy of the impossibility of tragedy, a
grimace of some otherworldly "high suffering". It is impossible to take seriously a
situation in which a man looks for the truth as if it were a toilet; contrariwise, he
may in actual fact be looking merely for a toilet and at the same time have the
impression that that is the truth and even justice (recall Mr. K in *The Trial*). It is
something ridiculous, absurd, trite, a sort of sleepy, boring meandering, and otherworldly.

The same heterogeneity is expressed, in a different key, in Kafka's metaphor of a universal inner ossification, in Gregor Samsa turning into a slippery
disgusting animal which he cannot shake off. Why is that? Why does one have to
resort to this kind of metaphor? Let me cite an example nearer home.

Can we apply, say, the concepts of courage and cowardice or sincerity
and insincerity to situations in which a "third", indescribable person finds himself, situations which can be referred to as "always too late". For instance, the
Russian tourist abroad was, until recently, precisely in such a situation. The criteria of cowardice and courage, sincerity and insincerity were inapplicable to him
for the simple reason that he found himself abroad on a specially arranged tour,
that is, enjoying a privilege of sorts, and it was therefore too late to display any
personal qualities. That is absurd, ridiculous.

The situation of the absurd is indescribable, it can only be conveyed
through the grotesque, through laughter. The language of good and evil, of courage and cowardice does not apply, since it lies entirely outside the domain delim-
ited by the acts of first containment. And language emerges precisely on the basis
of such acts.

Another example. Consider the Russian expression *kachat prava* (a
slangy phrase meaning to stand on one's rights, to fight against officialdom—Ed).
It applies to the actions of a person who seeks justice in the framework of law.
But if all actions of that person are linked together by a situation which did not
include the primary act of law, his search for the latter (carried out in the language which we all have in common—I mean the Europeans—and which has
come down to us from Montesquieu, Montaigne, Rousseau, from Roman law, and
so on) has no bearing on this situation. In fact, living in one situation, we have
often tried, and are still trying, to understand it in terms of quite another, starting
on and traversing the path followed by Mr. K in *The Trial*. Indeed, if we speak of
the seeds of the mind, one can also imagine the hair of the mind. Imagine that
man's hair on the head grows in instead of out; imagine a brain overgrown with
hair, where thoughts wander about as in a forest never finding one another, and

none of them being able to take shape. That is the primitive state of civic thought. Civilisation is in the first place the nation's spiritual health, and one therefore must be cautious above all not to damage it and make the concatenation of the consequences irreversible .

We are thus dealing with indeterminate situations and situations of the first two K's which have the same language. On this basis, we shall now define consciousness as the difference which undoubtedly exists and which is inexpressible through nomination of itself, being hidden behind the similarity and identity of nominations. Consciousness is precisely the elusive, outwardly indistinguishable and inexpressible element which distinguishes, e.g. the word "courage" in these situations. Consciousness is the distinction itself, the differentiatedness in the ontological sense.

THE FORMAL STRUCTURE OF CIVILISATION

To advance in our understanding of the links between consciousness and civilisation let us recall another law, formulated by Descartes, which has a bearing on all human states, including those in which the causal connectedness of world events is formulated. Descartes said that one has to hold on to a thought for a while, for thought itself is movement and there is no guarantee that one thought may be followed by another on the strength of some intellectual act or mental link. All that exists must *surpass* itself to be itself in the next moment of time. In content, the time of thought is discrete: what I am now does not follow from what I was before, and what I shall be tomorrow, or the next moment, does not follow from what I am now. It follows that the thought which will exist in the next moment of time will be there not because its beginning or a piece of it exists now. That is the way human being is structured, according to Descartes.

Civilisation is a mode of ensuring such containments. It is a formal device ensuring a system of distancing from concrete meanings and contents, or a system creating the space of realisation and a chance for thought starting at moment A being thought at moment B, or for a human state begun at moment A being a human .state at moment B. Let me cite an example.

There is today a sort of rapture about specialist thinking. It is believed to be thought as such, implemented by itself, as it were. Art and any other spheres of the so-called spiritual creativity may be said to belong to this isolated thinking. But the ability to think is not a privilege of some profession. In order to think, one must be able to gather together things unconnected for most men, and hold them together, collected, over a certain period of time. Regrettably, most men are still, as ever, as at any moment of human history, capable of very little by themselves, and know nothing except for the accidents of representations. They can only break animals' trails through the forest of vague images and concepts, and connect them in an indeterminate mass.

But, according to the first K principle ("I can"), in order to hold on to thought, one must have the "muscles of thought", the living strength (knowledge is power!) built up on the basis of certain first acts. In other words, trails of *coherent* space for thought must be broken, and these are the trails of *glasnost* (openness), debate, mutual tolerance, and formal law and order. It is this law and order that creates space and time for the freedom of interpretation, for *one's own* trial. There is the law of being named by one's own proper name, the law of nomination. It is a condition of historical force, an element of its form. Form is in fact the only structure in the world that requires freedom for adults, too. It may be said in this sense that laws, the real essence and state of affairs, exist only for free beings. Human institutions (and thought is also an institution) is the labour and patience of freedoms, there are no any other formulas. As long as you labour and think, civilisation ensures this, so that something might be set in motion and resolved, so that sense might be established, and you might learn what you thought, what you wanted, and what you felt. The mechanism of civilisation is the giving of a chance. It is an organised and structured assumption of this chance-giving.

By this fact civilisation assumes therefore the presence in it of cells of the unknowable. If there is no play left to the manifestation of not-entirely-known, civilisation, as well as culture (which is, in fact, one and the same thing) disappear. Thus the economic culture of production (i.e. not just the material production of finite wealth dying in the act of its use) signifies the unjustifiableness of a structure of government which decides when the peasant will sow, and covers the entire space of his activity by the distribution of such knowledge. I repeat that there must be free play allowed to accommodate the appearance in some areas of things which we do not know and cannot know beforehand, which we cannot assume to exist in some omniscient head.

One more example. Marx said that about as many stupid things had been said about money as about the nature of love. Let us assume, though, that the nature of money is unknown and is fixed in a formal civilisation mechanism, that men have assimilated money as culture to such an extent that money can be used to produce something, not just counted. Why is that possible? For the simple reason that it is assumed in this case that the exchange of money for a purchased product does not in its turn require time, since labour time is already embodied in money. Such behaviour is civilised. Such an abstraction is secured by civilisation itself, by a civilised structure of daily life, whereas behaviour that looks like it but comes from behind the looking-glass is uncivilised. In the absence of a cultured mechanism of money, there appears and exists behind-the-looking-glass behaviour involving money: if, say, 30 rubles have been earned (i.e. eight hours of labour have been put into earning a 30-ruble banknote as a sign) and an additional

10 hours have to be wasted, i.e. nearly 40 additional rubles, in order to spend them. The concept of money as value is, of course, absent in such consciousness. We cannot in this case compute the expenditures involved in the economy by using signs of signs, we cannot organise a rational scheme of economic production. And all the while we use money as signs and, moreover, having once found ourselves in this behind-the-looking-glass money world with apparently the same objects, we have squared the circle, having somehow become self seeking and cunning without knowing the value of money.

Civilisation thus presupposes formal mechanisms of ordered, lawful behaviour, not those based on someone's favour, idea or goodwill. That is a condition of social, civic thinking. "Even if we are enemies, let us behave in a civilised fashion, let us not hack at the branch on which we perch". The very essence of civilisation, of cultured and legal, suprasituational behaviour can be expressed in this simple sentence. Staying within the situation, it is impossible to agree not to harm each other ever, since it will always be "clear" to someone that he must restore violated justice. No evil has been committed in history without this kind of clear passion, for any evil often results from the best of intentions, and this is a far from ironical phrase. The energy of evil flows from the energy of the truth, of confidence in the vision of the truth. Civilisation blocks this, it delays this to an extent to which we human beings are in general capable of it.

In short, the destruction, the breaking off of the civilisation threads along which man's consciousness might have the time to arrive at the crystallisation of the truth (and the truth, as we know, is not inferred through deduction, since one has to hold on to the truth, since civilisation offers a chance to do so— and this chance is not just for the heroes of thought), destroys man, too. When all the formal mechanisms are eliminated under the banner of this-worldly perfection precisely on the grounds that they are formal and thus abstract compared to the immediate human reality, and easily criticisable, men deprive themselves of the possibility of being men, that is, of having an undisintegrated consciousness, not only sign consciousness .

MONOPOLY

Let me cite another example of such disintegration. It is a well-known fact that a system known as monopoly stands outside civilisation, for it destroys the very body of civilisation, giving rise to total devastation of the human world— not just in the sense that monopoly encourages the most primitive and asocial instincts, and creates channels for their manifestation. As I have noted, the state of thought arrived at must go through a "green run" in some agora-like space, building muscle in it, as a snowman gathers snow and thus gain strength for implementing its possibility. If there is no agora, of something that is developed, there is no truth.

Although man has faced, since time immemorial, the task of taming the savageness, fierceness, and egoism of his own nature, his instincts, greed, the darkness of his heart, soullessness and ignorance are quite capable of accommodating mental abilities, the intellect, and of realising themselves through them. And only the citizen who has the right to reason in his own mind, and who uses that right, can withstand that. And this right or law can only exist if the means of attaining the goals are in their turn legal, i.e. if they dissolve in themselves the spirit of law. In other words, they are concrete, embodied existences of men, instruments and utensils of life proceeding *from law* in themselves, actively present everywhere in whatever law can have a bearing on and what is regulated by law. Law cannot be implemented by arbitrary or administrative, i.e. extralegal means, even if we are guided in the process by the best of intentions and high considerations or "ideas". For its applications then spread the precedent and model of lawlessness contained in such means. (The broader and tougher applications, the broader and more painful the precedent and the model.) All this regardless of the intentions and ideals "for the benefit of" and "for the salvation of" or, on the contrary, out of evil design. This is obvious in the case of any monopoly. Let me put it this way. If, out of the highest considerations of social weal, I can one fine day fix a special price on certain goods, if I can conceal and secretly redistribute incomes, appoint privileges, distribute goods, if I can change, for the sake of planned targets, previous contracts with the working people, etc., etc., on that very day (and later, along an eternal parallel), the same will be done by somebody and somewhere (or by the same people and in the same place) out of quite different considerations: for personal gain, through profiteering, fraud, violence, stealing, bribery. The concrete causes and motives in the structures are indifferent, mutually replaceable, they flow into each other and can be transfigured into each other, for law is the same and indivisible at all points of space and time in which men act and are connected with each other. Including the laws of social weal. The goals of laws are thus achieved only through laws! If the latter are violated, one of the reasons is that law and order are replaced by the order of ideas, of "the truth", as if law existed by itself, outside human individuals and their understanding of what they do. It is impossible to do without the individual, without individual forces, without human development, without trust in elementary human common sense and personal convictions, and in ability to act on them. It is made impossible by the laws of being themselves, if they are to be distinguished from legal norms! That is the whole point. The possibility to bypass the individual is ruled out by virtue of the immutable structure of being itself, of life itself (if anything is to exist at all), rather than by virtue of humanist preference or care for man. Only at the level of men's existential equality can anything happen. Nothing is anyone's *due* here; we must all traverse the path ourselves, and perform our own movement "in the middle of our nature", as our famous poet Derzhavin wrote once upon a time. Without this movement there are no external attainments and no institutions. Without this movement, the entire production of the truth will be destroyed, its ontological basis and nature will be destroyed, and lies will prevail—lies produced by other causes yet extrahuman and total, taking up all the points of social space and filling them with signs. The play in the mirrors, surreal-sign reflection of something else will prevail.

THE WORLD BEHIND THE LOOKING–GLASS

Of course, the emergence of such a behind-the-looking-glass game is connected with its inherent behind-the-looking-glass meanings; the impression is that they indeed possess some kind of higher wisdom. The fact is that people in this game see the whole. In their view, the external observer is always wrong. Let us recall Gottfried Benn's words: "The whole belongs only to you."

One observer sees what is being destroyed, another, what is being built, while many look on, winking at one another: we know what is happening, "we have access to the whole". That is what the "inner" things are. To me, though, this inner life immersed in itself, without an agora, is the same as looking for the truth in the toilet. If I had the talent of Kafka, I would describe this search within the soul as a strange, fantastic search for the truth in an area in which it simply cannot exist according to the ontological laws of human being.

Men of indeterminate situations, or of total sign other being, remind me in this sense of those whom Friedrich Nietzsche called "the last men"— for a good reason. Indeed, his uneasy Christian conscience cried out that we shall either be supermen, in order to *be men* (the first two K-principles are the principles of man's transcendence towards the human in man himself), or we shall prove to be "the last men". We shall be men of organised happiness who cannot even despise ourselves, living as we do in a situation of destroyed consciousness and destroyed matter of the human.

Therefore, if human events take place somewhere, they cannot take place without participation of consciousness; consciousness cannot be eliminated from these events or reduced to something else. This consciousness is dual in the following fundamental sense. In introducing the K-principles, I actually specified two intersecting planes. One was the plane of what I called ontology (it cannot be anyone's actual experience but it nevertheless is; for instance, death cannot be this kind of experience, but the *symbol* of death is a productive element of human conscious life). The second, "muscular" or real plane, is the, ability to live under that symbol in actual fact, on the basis of acts of first containment. Neither of these planes can be ignored: consciousness is fundamentally dual. Behind the looking-glass, though, where left and right switch places, all meanings are turned upside down, and the destruction of human consciousness begins. The anomalous sign space swallows everything that comes in contact with it. Human consciousness disappears, and, finding himself in a situation of indeterminateness, where all and everything exchange winks, not just ambiguous ones, but winks implying a wide range of meanings, man disappears, too: there is no courage, no honour, no cowardice, and no dishonour left. These "conscious" acts and knowledge cease to participate in world events, in history. It does not matter what is there in your consciousness—all you have to do is give a sign. In the limit, the need for the most vital thing disappears—the need for men to have any convictions. It does not matter whether you believe in what is happening or not, for it is precisely by giving the sign that you are included in the action and in the working of the wheels of the social mechanism.

In 20th-century literature, such situations were fully realised. I refer not only to Franz Kafka here but also to Robert Musil, the author of *The Man Without Qualities*. Musil saw clearly that in the situation prevailing in the Austro-Hungarian empire, teetering on the brink of collapse, whatever one might attempt to do would result in some kind of balderdash—simply because it is *too late*. Whether you look for the truth or for the untruth, you will follow the already pre-determined path of absurdity. He knew well that acting and thinking *within* such a situation was impossible: it was important to get out of it.

Not to force the reader to think too seriously on some of my terms (and I mean the terms only, not the problems; some serious thinking must be done on the problems, while my terms are not obligatory at all), I shall express my experience of "behind-the-looking-glass existence" as follows. The whole of my "theory" of consciousness may be reduced to a single seed in one early emotional experience—the first impression from the point at which civilisation on the one hand and blank life on the other meet. I felt that my attempt to remain human in this situation was grotesque, ridiculous. The foundations of civilisation were undermined to such an extent that it was impossible to bring into the open, discuss and contemplate one's own diseases. The less we could bring them into the open, the more they germinated, remaining in the depth, and we were overtaken by a secret, imperceptible decay brought about; by the decline of civilisation, by the absence of the agora.

In 1917, a rotten regime collapsed, and the dust and soot of the rotten vast structure still haunt us. The world is still full of victims waiting to be mourned for, it is flooded with blood waiting to be atoned for. The fates of many who died nobody knows what for, cry out for the meaning of what has happened. It is one thing to die completing and, by one's death, establishing, for the first time, a certain meaning (e.g. in the struggle for freedom), and it is quite a different thing to vanish while blindly running wild, so that the meaning has to be still searched for, when blood begins to ooze here and there, like the blood on the tombstones of righteous men in legends, in completely unexpected places and without any comprehensible reason.

We still live as distant heirs of that "radiation sickness", more terrible, in my view, than any Hiroshima; strange heirs, who have understood very little, and have been taught very little by our own misfortunes. These are generations that have produced no offspring, so to speak, for that which has not been born, which has not created in itself the **soil** and the vital force for germination, is incapable of bearing offspring. So now we wander from country to country, without a language, our memory confused, our history rewritten, not knowing at times what actually took place, and is taking place, in and around ourselves; claiming no right to a knowledge of freedom and responsibility for making use of it. Unfortunately, today, as before, vast isolated spaces on the earth are taken up by this behind-the-looking-glass antiworld.

That is why, whenever I hear of ecological disasters, possible cosmic conflicts, nuclear war, radiation sickness or AIDS, all this seems to me to be less terrible and more remote (I may be mistaken, and my imagination may be too feeble) than the things that I have described, and which are in actual fact the most terrible catastrophe, for it involves the human element itself. Its fate determines everything else, it determines whether what I have described here Will happen.

Let me recall here that Lake Baikal was "safe and sound" when, as early as the **1920s,** and later, we were already confronted with the horrible spectacle of man's degenerate face; the newcomers from behind the looking-glass, who can only be imagined as an exotic crossing between rhinoceros and locust, filled the whole space and intertwined in an ugly round-dance, sowing death and the stupor of inexplicable doom. I began with verse; let me end with verse, too: "Hunchbacked and nocturnal, they carry on their shoulders the silences of slippery obscurity and the sandstorms of fear."[1]

---

[1] F. Garcia Lorca, "Romance de la Guardia Civil espanola", *Obras completas,* Vol. 1, Bilbao, 1974, p. 426.

KOLMOGOROV AS HISTORIAN

Valentin Yanin[1]

When talking to his disciples Andrei Kolmogorov, a famous Soviet mathematician, reminisced of his first steps in science which were made not only in mathematics but also in history when while being a participant in the seminar conducted by historian S. Bakhrushin he studied Novgorodian cadastres. It was believed that the works themselves had not been preserved but after the demise of Kolmogorov manuscripts of his historical studies were discovered in his archives.

Four preserved manuscripts of Kolmogorov which are devoted to the history of Novgorod reflect both the final result of his studies and the preparatory stages which were apparently approved during the discussions at the seminar. The draft versions are represented by manuscripts A ("Landownership in Novgorodian *piatinas*[2] in the 15th Century. Part One") and B ("Novgorod, Drafts: On Collection of Revenues from Land Tenure"). The first manuscript marked "Completed on January 14, 1921" concludes the research part by a summary of conclusions. The second one, which is not dated but is titled by the author as a draft, presents materials which were included in an enlarged form into the final version of the study.

This final version is contained in manuscripts C ("Novgorodian *Land-ownership* in the 15th Century. Part One") and D which does not have a title. The two manuscripts form a single whole although designation "Part One" appears only in manuscript C which has a chronological mark "November 1920-February 1921". This part provides final formulation of the ideas that underlie draft manuscript A dated January 14, 1921. Presumably, the first part took its final shape

---

[1] V. Yanin, Corr. Mem., AS, head of the Chair of Archaeology at the Department of History of Moscow State University, specialist in the history and archaeology of Old Russia. Author of many works in the field, including the books: *Deed Seals of Old Rus* (in two volumes); *The Novgorod Feudal Estates:* and *Novgorod Posadniks*.

[2] In cadastres the Novgorodian land was divided into 5 fiscal parts called piatinas

after the January discussion of this section of the work. Draft B was used in the final version of the second part of the study (in manuscript D) dated January 15, 1922.

We may assume that the work on the first part of the study dates back to November 1920-February 1921 while the author started work on the second part in the spring of 1921 and completed it at the very beginning of 1922. In November 1920 Kolmogorov was seventeen and a half years old while in January 1922 he was under nineteen .

Andrei Kolmogorov on more than one occasion told his disciples of the end of his "carrier as historian". When the work was presented by him at the seminar the head of the seminar Professor Bakhrushin while approving the results noted however that the conclusions of the young researcher cannot claim to be final because in historical science every conclusion should be based on several proofs. Later recalling this Kolmogorov added that he decided to devote himself to a science which needed only one proof for the final conclusion. Thus, history lost a talented scholar while mathematics gained him finally.

Young Kolmogorov chose cadastres of the Novgorodian land of the late 15th-early 16th centuries as the object of his studies. This source has no parallel for the reconstruction of economic history of the 15th-century Novgorod. Throughout the 1480s the Grand Prince Ivan III, who joined Novgorod to Moscow in January 1478, undertook an action of unprecedented scope by transferring Novgorodian peasants to Nizovskie[3] lands and repopulating them by Nizovskie people (from Moscow, Kostroma, Kolomna and other towns) who came into possession of former estates of Novgorodian citizens. By undertaking this action Moscow laid down the foundation for a single economic system of the emerging united national Russian state.

The first cadastre of Novgorodian lands was prepared about 1492 (this date was once again substantiated by Kolmogorov contrary to the opinion of some experts). This cadastre, which has not reached our times, contained lists of all big and small estates with the indication of date concerning owners resettled from Novgorod, profitability of *volostoks,* volumes of quit-rent and taxes and descriptions of the new owners of these lands. We can leaf only through the pages of the books of the second variant which was started not earlier than 1495 and contained references to the first cadastre as the "old variant."

The books of the second variant, while preserving the above-mentioned principles of land description, contain consequently two chronological cross-sections and graphically reflect the dynamics of the historical process at the most important stage of Moscow's development of the Novgorodian heritage. By the

---

[3] Nizovskielands are lands of the Vladimir-Suzdal and other southern, with respect to Novgorod, principalities called "niz" (low lands) or nizovskie lands.

early 1920s study of cadastres had already had a noticeable historiography. Their studies began in the 1840s and were accompanied by the publication of the source itself. The main six-volume edition was started in 1859 and completed in 1910, in 1915 a reference section was added to it (which was prepared very carelessly). Some materials were published outside the main edition (which was not reflected in the reference section. Subsequent years witnessed publication (1930) of the cadastre of a number of *pogosts*[4] of the northern part of Obonezhskaya *piatina* and small extracts from the books of the second census were published from time to time.

In other words, Kolmogorov had already had at his disposal a considerable amount of materials which enabled him to make an assessment of the qualitative condition of the source and the level of preceding research work on it which was carried out with the participation of prominent scholars, for instance, K. Nevolin, V. Klyuchevsky, A. Nikitsky, A. Gnevushev, A. Andriyashev and B. Grekov.

When assessing the historiographic place of Kolmogorov's studies it is necessary first of all to pay attention to the striking independence of thought which is not usually typical of young humanitarian researchers. This independent attitude had an impact not only on the future choice of profession but also on accurate characteristics of preceding studies. Kolmogorov highly valued historico-geographical aspect present in the study of cadastres in the works of Nevolin and Andriyashev; he was upset by the habit of mixing facts relating to different parts of Russia which obliterated local specific features of regions (in the works of Klyuchevsky, I. Belyaev and V: Sergeyevich); use of individual facts from cadastres suitable for the occasion in the works of Nikitsky; specific conclusions of Grekov who unjustifiably used later materials for reconstructing earlier and basically different periods. While giving tribute of respect to the works of Gnevushev Kolmogorov characterised them as a miscellany of unprocessed materials mainly in the form of tables and enumeration of facts, compiled, according to him, with considerable omissions and errors which did however exert a decisive influence on the conclusions.

The difficulties in studying cadastres are basically determined by several circumstances. It is quite apparent that the main difficulties would not have emerged if the cadastre books had been preserved in their exhaustive entirety. As a matter of fact, their completeness is very relative. Let alone the fact that many books have considerable omissions, I mean that even those books which have been preserved most fully do not contain description of all the *pogosts*. There is no description of the majority of the *pogosts* of Obonezhskaya *piatina* (by the

---

[4] Pogostswere administrative-fiscal units, centres of the Novgorodian land including the church and the cemetery.

time Kolmogorov studied this *piatina* only a small extract was published), there is no description of the considerable part of Bezhetsk *piatina*. Therefore a researcher seeking to make generalised observations, for instance, in assessing the total number of villages, estates, gross harvests or population of the Novgorodian land would apparently confront an insurmountable methodological barrier. The Novgorodian land by virtue of its vast territory includes areas with different landscape and climatic characteristics, with different types of farm management and eventually with different density of the population. In addition it is necessary to take into account that credibility of the majority of original elements of the study is debatable.

It is possible to avail of concrete examples in order to illustrate the difficulties of this kind. In their descriptions cadastres compute "people" in a homestead. Who of the dwellers of the homestead is designated by this term? Sergeyevich believed that adult men were covered by it. Gnevushev understood heads of families as "people". There are considerable differences in correlation of people and homesteads in one and the same estate according to the "old scribe" and according to the second census which may reflect a change in the content of this term rather than demographic dynamics. If cadastres compute only "people" by imparting a certain content to this notion, then what was—let it be even the average statistical calculation—the population of one homestead? It is absolutely clear that contingent on the solution of this basic question are such important operations as computations of population density in different regions and estimation of the total strength of the population. Basically speaking, the entire history and computations of cadastres, as it became apparent to Kolmogorov, represent a search for efficient methodology which was a kind of groping in a thick forest abundant in fellings, intractable moors and paths leading nowhere.

In his studies Kolmogorov acts in two hypostases reflecting his evolution both as a historian and a mathematician. The first part of his work is a purely historical composition which clarifies difficult and traditionally debatable problems inherent to the subject chosen for his study. It should be noted that in the draft version of this section (manuscript A) the author made an attempt to probe for a method to generalise the data for properly described *pogosts* in order to determine percentage correlation of lands belonging to different owners, assess population density and eventually on the basis of these parameters, different Novgorodian *piatinas* and the entire land as a whole. However this rather voluminous section was excluded from the final text of the study. It should be presumed that the researcher felt that he did not have enough basic data to make such responsible conclusions. While editing the final version of the work and assessing the credibility of cadastres he proceeded from the assumption that this credibility was sufficient only for tentative conclusions, that is the only possible conclusions in view of their incomplete nature. In other words, he studied thoroughly percentage correlation of categories of owners for each *piatina* and computed density of homesteads and not of population. (While qualifying this episode as a case of elementary statistical use of cadastre data we shall observe that the entire remaining part of the content of the first part of the study belongs to the sphere of traditionally historical methods and Kolmogorov brilliantly demonstrated that he commanded them well).

The system of Novgorodian landownership of the 15th century is described by him as an integral and thoroughly balanced concept which clearly proved interpretation of "people" as working people, he also substantiated the average statistical population of a homestead (5-6 persons) derived from the size of arable land and provided precise description of *boyars* and *svoezemtsy*.[5] Of principled importance is his criticism levelled at Grekov's tenet concerning the allegedly existing division of archbishop's lands into properly "archbishop's" lands and "attributed" lands. Grekov considered the former as personal estates of the archbishop while the latter—as "black" lands not entrusted to the *boyars* but to the archbishop as master of the Sophian, i.e. state, treasury. Kolmogorov demonstrated that phraseology did not conceal any difference and all the lands associated with the archbishop were "black".

Naturally it is possible to single out erroneous conclusions in this work, which are related to the general level of historical knowledge of the time but these conclusions always remain at the far end of the concept without affecting its content. It is important to draw attention to another element. In some of the particular subjects which are raised only in passing in connection with the general concept without any detailed elaboration the author, so to speak, foresees things many years ahead. For instance, he takes notice but does not provide explanation to the similarity of organisational structures in archbishop's lands and Yuriev monastery's *volosts (volosts* of other monasteries were structurally different). As a matter of fact, it became known only recently that the Yuriev monastery played a special role in the system of organisation of the black clergy; its Father Superior was the archimandrite of Novgorod who was elected like other city councils at the *veche* (assembly) and consequently like the archbishop headed an important sphere of state life. When considering priests' lands Kolmogorov paid attention to the exceptional nature of the city's St. Michael's church whose *volost* numbered 422 homesteads. Indeed it is a highly exceptional case: delegation of lands from the composition of Novgorod pogosts to the prince's church apparently occurred following the conflict of the 1270s when unauthorised allocation of *pogost* lands to this church was described in the treaty between Novgorod and Prince Yaroslav Yaroslavich as an unlawful act.

---

[5] Svoezemtsy were petty feudal lords who had not been removed from their possessions by Ivan 111.

Some of the observations of Kolmogorov are capable of shedding light on the sources which were discovered many decades after he conducted his study. Thus, he paid particular attention to cases of deception of scribes from whom concerned owners concealed data on actual size of their incomes. In 1959 birch-bark scroll No. 359 dating back to the turn of the 1 5th century was found in Novgorod. Comparison of the texts leads to the conclusion about the identity of actions and consequently similar methods of bookkeeping already at the time of Novgorod rule, almost one hundred years before Novgorod lost its independence.

If as far back as early 1921 Kolmogorov as a researcher was still a "pure" historian then the accomplished result of his study provides the most graphic identification of the drawback of the traditional method as well as the presence of a whole range of problems which did not emerge if the customary pattern of regular historiographic controversies was followed. When initiating the work on the second part of his study he concentrated his attention, already in a small draft, on absolutely new—in terms of the study of Novgorodian sources—problems whose solution required a strictly mathematical approach. These problems are clearly formulated by Kolmogorov in the methodological section of the manuscript completed by the beginning of 1922:

"Firstly, thanks to the fact that in the books we find not only the totals but also the enumeration of all cases, it opens up broad opportunities for combined computations clarifying not only the average dimensions but also fluctuations and relationship of phenomena (see, for instance, further relation between *obzha*[6] taxation and volume of hay-making). Then, it is possible to subject to statistical investigation the data which were not designed for this purpose, for instance, names. Finally, it is also possible to arrive at very interesting results by using more specific properties of figures. Here is an example of such investigation: determination of the procedure for collecting taxes on incomes of private owners by the multiple of the figures for homesteads or *obzhas,* etc. These problems have been barely touched upon by Gnevushev. It is precisely the use of these somewhat more refined methods that unites my present work. These methods can be used for studying other cadastres."

The author used the probability theory as the basis for his method, which was not applied to Novgorodian cadastres before him and which, unfortunately, has not been used until today because the researchers were not aware of Kolmogorov's work written nearly seventy years ago. "The main method of the final section (IV— *'Obzha* Taxation')," wrote Kolmogorov, "represents the establishment of a certain regularity in figures; for instance, a great number of settlements with round number of *obzhas,* or coincidence between fractions of *obzhas* of the

---

[6] Obzha was a unit of taxation

old scribe with the relatively seldom case of their presence in *vopchie*[7] villages. Such a regularity may occur incidentally but its probability is exceptionally small, in the study cases it equals to about 1/1000th, while at the same time its explanation by other reasons is not so far from this probability; it gives us the possibility to affirm that in accordance with the well-known theorem of the probability theory the presence of high probability of these reasons—in the present cases exceeding 99/100th and in the case of the latter use concerning non-applicability of fraction-wise taxation of large villages exceeding 999/1000th—is tantamount to credibility for historical conclusions".

The work also raises and settles a number of specific problems having fundamental importance. First of all Kolmogorov considered the problem of population concentration in some areas of the Novgorodian land. In all Novgorodian *pogosts* (with the exception of cases having apparent explanation) sizes of settlements ranged from 1.7 to 5 homesteads per settlement. As a matter of fact, in Yamskoy, Koporsky and, in part, Korelsky districts their number per settlement increases from 6 to 10.7. Gnevushev explained this concentration by development of trades, e.g. iron-works and fishing; Kolmogorov graphically demonstrated that it was not so and that concentration of population was linked to frontline location of these *pogosts.*

With regard to the most difficult question concerning the content of the term " people" applied to the population registered by the cadastre Kolmogorov convincingly refutes opinions of his predecessors and substantiates the idea that the number of "people" included all working population, or at least a category of people much broader than just heads of families. This conclusion is substantiated by a comparison between the number of "people" in a homestead and the size of the arable land whose increase was far from being proportionate to the growth in the number of people: if the term "people" denominated only heads of families, then, naturally, the volume of ploughed land would have reflected presence of two, three or more families, which was not the case.

In this connection turning once again to the probability theory the researcher suggests a most ingenious method to determine the number of relatives and non-relatives in settlements relying on the coincidence of patronymics and names of the dwellers in homesteads for those cases when the degree of kinship or presence of kinship among the dwellers was not directly indicated in the cadastres. By thoroughly analysing materials for a number of major settlements of Karagalsky *pogost* of the Koporsky district he came to the conclusion that one-third of the inhabitants were related by kin to somebody among two neighbouring entries in the cadastre: this fact, in his opinion, is more important than permissible accidental coincidences. More precise calculations enabled Kolmogorov to

---

[7] Vopchie were villages in which the lands belonged to different owners. 120

assert that in the same district at least half of the homesteads in settlements numbering 10 homesteads or more were related by kin to some of the dwellers of the same settlement.

The result obtained on the basis of this investigation led the researcher to important conclusions of general historical nature. It was found that in Shelonskaya and in greater part of Vodskaya *piatinas* the majority of villages were of very old origin with established and hardly extendable dimensions of arable lands which led to the diffusion of the population, formation of *pochinoks*[8] or migration of peasants to other villages with available plots whereas Derevskaya *piatina* had a considerable number of villages which emerged recently and were expanding. This process of vigorously developing colonisation is more conspicuous in the remote Bezhetskaya *piatina*.

Undoubtedly the concluding section of Kolmogorov's work *"Obzha Taxation"* represents its pinnacle. *Obzha* as a unit of taxation still continues to attract attention of researchers. In order to answer the question whether *obzha is* a measure of arable land, or a measure of qualitative assessment of land, or a measure of work, or, finally, a measure of availability of draught animals in a homestead it is possible to proceed from the assumption, (for the first time noticed by Kolmogorov) what—a settlement or a homestead—served as an initial unit of taxation. In other words, whether each homestead was taxed first and the total determined the amount of taxation for the entire settlement or vice versa, first the settlement was taxed and then the sum was divided among the homesteads. As the number of homesteads in a settlement often exceeds its *obzha* taxation, the homesteads were to be assessed with a fraction number of *obzhas*. But in this case the total sum of taxations should have a fractioned number in at least half of the cases. But the materials analysed by the researcher demonstrate the opposite: a settlement usually had a round number of *obzhas* and consequently it was the village rather than the homestead that was taxed. In developing his analysis Kolmogorov discovered that totals of taxation for *volostoks* gravitated towards round figures. He constantly came across "totals" like 10, 15, 20 whereas figures like 13, 16, 19, etc. cropped up very seldom. This observation led him to think that when imposing *obzhas* the scribes took guidance from their own observations rather than old documents. This conclusion is corroborated by the dynamics of *obzha* taxation when changes in the imposed sums were not caused by changes in the size of arable lands or other components of the estate. Thus, indices of profitability of the estate expressed in the amount of the quit-rent appeared to be more important for correct assessment of the value of an estate.

Of great importance are Kolmogorov's observations contained in his study which relate to parallel existence of homestead-wise and head-wise taxa-

---

[8] Pochinoks means new villages having temporary benefits and freed from taxation.

tion. The latter seems to be a real relic which was confirmed by birch-bark scroll No. 663 of the turn of the 13th century found in 1985 in Novgorod. According to this scroll the sum of tax payments for a family of three correlates to the sum of taxes for a family of two as 3: 2 .

Later studies of the Novgorodian land cadastres continued without the participation of Kolmogorov whose work was not published and remained unknown for the researchers. The *votchina* economy of Novgorodian landowners of the times of independence is described in the works of S. Tarakanova-Belkina, L. Danilova, V. Yanin and other researchers. A three-volume generalised work *Agrarian History of Russia's North-West* prepared by a team of Leningrad scholars headed by A. Shapiro was published in 19711978. In considering these works through the prism of impressions from young Kolmogorov's work it is possible to state with regret that despite all the merits of these works they develop the traditional method of source-study analysis and naturally improve but do not revolutionise it. If the work of the famous mathematician had been published shortly after it was written our knowledge would have been fuller today and what matters most it would have been more precise. Publication of this work is still necessary today because it directs the mind of researchers to the still untapped historiographic problems and arms them with precise methodology.

Kolmogorov's works on history which are being prepared for press by the History Department of Moscow University should be published in all their entirety, including the drafts and preparatory materials. It will provide the readers with the opportunity not only to see the evolution of the research thought of the author. Part of his reflections still relevant today was not included in the final text. Naturally, they should be accompanied with commentaries which will make it possible to compare the road suggested by Kolmogorov and the road followed by researchers during the past seventy years.

SOCIAL HISTORY AND HISTORICAL SCIENCE

Aron Gurevich[1]

The present situation in the science of history in this country allows contradictory comments. On the one hand, the pressure that for many years was deforming scientific quest and the minds of researchers has been lifted. Today, they can freely discuss the recent taboos and make public any conclusions invited by their studies. Today, the post-October period is emerging in a new light. So far, such comments and conclusions are nothing more than mere declarations of future profound archival research on the fundamental historical problems. At this stage, however, these declarations are very important.

On the other hand, historians stubbornly ignore that fact that history's grave and persistent disease was not caused by censorship alone. It is an illusion to think that freedom of thought guarantees science's rapid progress. The deforming disease cut deeply into history's methodology and the theory of research the key to many locks. For many decades the methodology of scientific research has been restricted by militant dogmatism all restrictions should be removed and the methodology should be revised together with the range of problems and themes.

At the turn of the 60s there was a lively discussion of history's theoretical and philosophical aspects, a certain impact of which can be felt till this day. General stagnation in social and intellectual life could not but distort theoretical quest in the humanities. Time has come to raise these problems once more—however, this should be a dramatic advance rather than a return to the original point of

---

[1] **A. Gurevich,** D. Sc. (Hist.), senior researcher of the Institute of World History, AS. Specialist in mediaeval culture. Author of books: *Categories of Mediaeval Culture; Problems of Mediaeval Folk Culture, Problems of Genesis of Feudalism in Western Europe.*

departure. The advance movement should reflect the current shifts in science and public consciousness.

The fundamental concepts of the social sciences, including history, are prone to change—they are not immutable and depend on the experience accumulated both by the sciences of man and society. This explains why an analysis of new experience is indispensable for any revision of the conceptual and methodological apparatus used by the humanities today. In the context of the coming renovation of history methodological discussions are inevitable and very important.

Historical science today cannot but lean on social history that is emerging as the central line of research. We cannot refrain from its content and orientation. It should be noted, however, that social history was mainly interpreted as socioeconomic history. It is concerned with society's class structure, social and property differentiation, the form of exploitation and the contradictions they bred, the class antagonisms, the structure of land tenure and organisation of agricultural production, of handicrafts and industry. In Marxist historiography research subjects stem from the concept of the mode of production and are chosen to clarify its development.

The distance between the subject of political economy and sociology, on the one hand, and the subject of historical research proper, on the other, is frequently ignored. This leads to a situation when a vast body of specific observations and constructs of social history for a long time illustrated historical materialism rather than investigated its own subject. This deprived historical process of its colour and many dimensions.

I would like to add in this connection that this confusion of the philosophy of history and the historical science proper resulted in an inadequate attention to the special methodology of historical knowledge designed to clarify the system of methods applicable to history and patterned according to its specificity. Works by I. Kovalchenko[1] and J. Topolski[2] are rare exceptions from this rule.

A shift from the realm of universal categories and the theory of the world historical process to the realm of applied methodology and the theories of the "average level" that exist outside extreme generalisations and actively absorb and process results of research is a *sine qua non* of a tailored methodology of historical knowledge. It is expedient, therefore, to generalise the practice of a historian's craftsmanship and the living experience of historians to reveal the inner logic of their procedures and to identify the leading trends in historical thought and its contemporary orientations rather than to provide historians with prescriptions and abstract norms.

It is not my intention to discuss a certain special historical methodology in its general form. Here I shall discuss certain approaches to social history that have become evident as this century is drawing to its end. I am not aiming at a survey of contemporary historiography abroad. My aim is to identify the basic methodological prerequisites that guide historians and to hypothesize the concept of social history's enrichment and deepening. Hence my attention to the following aspects:

1. An analysis of the conceptual apparatus of social-historical research.
2. Difficulties of interpreting social history that stems from its traditional interpretation, and attempts to overcome them.

My discussion mostly rests on materials pertaining to mediaeval Europe though I believe that my observations can be applied to a wider range of problems. One should bear in mind that the general problems of historical epistemology were mainly discussed within the framework of historiography of the New Time as applied to the Middle Ages and partly Classical Antiquity. They have come to their ends that allows historians to take them as a whole and to use them as a sort of a laboratory for discussing general historical concepts.

I.

It is very important to distinguish between the concepts used by social historians. Some of them are borrowed from contemporary social reality, rather than from the past and the written sources. Naturally, historians cannot avoid using them. Here I have in mind the general concepts of "class", "society", "state", "property" and "socio-economic formation". They (and similar general typological definitions) are freely applied to all ages and epochs. Even if they are not inclined to use this range of concepts indiscriminately and outside the period's specifics historians should be aware that they are introducing ideas that totally belong to modern sociology. The question arises whether these and similar concepts can be adequately applied to the past.

Here are recent examples. In her works on the early Roman society E. Staerman voices her doubts that the social groups of the patricians and plebeans in Ancient Rome can be described as classes and consequently this period of the early Roman history as an early class. Therefore, she is inclined to reject the presence of the state in royal and republican Rome.[3]

Here is another example. While Soviet specialists in the Middle Ages insist that feudalism and the classes of lords and dependent peasants were emerging in the early Middle Ages some contemporary French historians argue that the turn of the 11th century witnessed a feudal revolution and that in the preceding period there were no classes. Feudalism itself invites different opinions:

can it be widely interpreted so that it would fit different societies or should it be applied only to some West European countries?[4]

It is not my aim to discuss different points and take sides; the general sociological concepts of "class", "state" or "property" (either slave-owning or feudal) are nothing but conceptual instruments used by a contemporary historian.

Modern historical science cannot avoid using them. Still, they allow different interpretations and their use in historical science is sometimes open to doubt.

This is but one row of historical-sociological concepts that can be described as macrohistorical. There is another set of concepts designated as microhistorical—"family", "clan", "tribe", "community", "parish", "estate", "inherited estate", "corporation", "guild", "fraternity", "the circle of seigneurs and vassals" and so on. Here I limit myself with the Middle Ages though the list can be easily extended. As distinct from macrosociological concepts the presence of which is proved by indirect data the existence of microgroups is, as a rule, registered directly in historical sources.

Strictly speaking, the macrosociological concepts can be detected in historical sources as well. This requires a detailed analysis, however.

Such were, for example, three "estates" in a highly original sociological pattern that had taken shape in Mediaeval Latin works. In the first third of the 11th century there appeared writings of the highest clergy in France presenting a three function pattern of Christian society—God's triple house that was headed by the monarch and consisted of three ordines, those of praying, fighting and working (or landtilling). A superficial observer might take it as reflecting the social system of feudal Europe: the clergy and monks, knights and peasants. This pattern survived till the New Time and was reflected in the three estates of the Etats généraux. A closer look, however, will tell that far from describing the sociopolitical realities, it perpetrated definite ideology. J. Duby[5] and J. Le Goff are convinced that this ideology was intended to underpin monarchy. They argue that each "ordine" had a function to perform without which the whole (monarchy or society) could not survive. What we have here is an "imaginary world" rather than a copy of reality: urban population was left outside it.

In this way, the heuristic status of the macro- and microsociological concepts in history differs—the micro-sociological concepts are verified by the sources rather than postulated by the researcher (this situation does not do away with a necessity of decoding and interpreting historical sources). Their empirical nature is higher than that of the macro-sociological categories, they are of different theoretical generalisation. The macrosociological categories' content is of a theoretical a priori nature. It reaches the highest level in the concepts of "slavery", "feudalism", "Asiatic mode of production" and similar descriptions of formations. It seems that traditionally we overestimate the significance of macrosociological categories and underestimate microsociology. While "inherited estates", "estates" and "corporations" got our attention the rest of similar concepts remained neglected. For example, Olga Dobiash-Rozhdestvenskaya[6] paid practically no attention to parish whose role in mediaeval Europe could hardly be overestimated. The same can be said about the monastic community and fraternity. Other social microorganisms, such as the family and its forms that were studied from the outside while they should have been studied from the inside as a closely knit worlds that ensured day-to-day life. Soviet historians concentrated on classes, estates and their conflicts while private life remained outside their scope.

I am not suggesting to cast aside all attempts at class analysis—the contrary is true: I am suggesting to deepen and concretise it by climbing down from the heights of macrosociology. The present trend towards local history that concerns itself with individual villages, towns, neighbourhoods or even families and their relations between themselves and other small groups can fill in the gap. Here, interesting phenomena can be found.

For example, E. Le Roy Ladurie, a prominent French historian, wrote about Montaillou,[7] a village in the Pyrenees. He studied its life at the turn of the 14th century and demonstrated that not the seigneur or the count and the bishop far removed from the mountainous village but the rivaling local clans headed by the wealthiest and socially influential leaders exerted the greatest influence on the villagers' daily life. These horizontal ties and relationships were more important than the vertical ties of domination and subjugation. We cannot extend these conclusions to the entire country. His observations, however, have shed light on the microcommunities' internal mechanisms that historians were unable to see. Not a single society consists solely of large classes: there are always numerous smaller communities inside it. It is a historian's duty to carefully single them out, to determine their places, their relations with macrogroups and their role in the general social macroprocesses. The forces of social cohesion are especially powerful at the level of macrogroups—the family, clan, fraternity, etc.—which adds significance to their studies. In Montaillou material dependence was only partially responsible for people's cohesion around one of two warring clans—they were the centres of social attraction and the points of concentration of personal power. They cemented interpersonal, family and emotional relationships.

Some of the social phenomena indistinguishable at the macrolevel are clearly seen at the microlevel. While the macroanalysis concerns itself with the typical, recurrent and mass phenomena, it lets out of its scope unique phenomena that are exceptions rather than parts of series. A closer look at the nature of such exceptions might disclose that they are manifestations of trends that historians fail to recognise at the level of macroanalysis. An exception develops into a rule and enriches the content of macrohistory. For many years the institute of exchanging gifts was believed to be limited to the primitive pre-class system. All mentions of it in the sources related to more complicated systems were ignored as insignificant archaic survivals. Later, it became clear that it was one of the most important social institutes in Mediaeval society that retained their significance in the New Time as well.[8]

In this way, microanalysis specifies observations at the macrolevel, modify and enrich them. It brings historians closer to man as the centre of their research.[9]

Let me now switch to another problem of social history that is coming to the fore in contemporary historiography.

In the conditions of the present fragmentation of historical knowledge into numerous particular disciplines it is hard to grasp the object of social history and to understand how it correlates with the history of economy, technology and science, law and culture. Historians of different schools offered different answers to this question. Here is how Trevelyan interpreted social history.[10] He put away the history of events and political history and never imparted much attention to the history of classes and other social groups. The British historian put, in fact, social history and the history of everyday life on the same ground by shifting his spotlight on the way of life, customs and habits, forms of dwellings and fashions. Indeed, these changeable elements of human life present great interest, historians should not ignore them. Is social life limited by them alone? What do they conceal? Trevelyan as an empirical historian disregarded this question: the mountain of striking facts buried the deep-going processes.

Trevelyan's tradition proved to be more viable than one was inclined to expect. It seems to me that Braudel's conception[11] belongs to the same row even if it is found at the opposite end of it. While unfolding a sweeping panorama of capitalism's material civilisation he limits himself to gathering facts—from the monetary systems and commodities turnover to minutest details of everyday life. He has never posed himself a task of looking for the internal meaning of facts he extracted from archives. This is all the more strange since for many years Braudel headed the Annales school the founders of which (Bloch and Febvre) described history as a problem. Marc Bloch was the greatest social historian of this century. He posed himself an ambitious aim to go deep to the human core of the material and spiritual processes he studied. He wanted to look at the entire feudal society at the levels of production, social relations and relations between classes and groups and social psychology. The main thrust of his research efforts was aimed at a synthesis of these levels that were reflected in social activity. Bloch regarded history as a "total" or "global" history, a history of people in society.[12] Braudel lacks this pathos of historical synthesis.

Meanwhile, this is the gist of the problem. How can we close the gap between the social and economic structures, on the one hand, and the mental and spiritual structures, on the other, that revealed itself in historical studies and how can we expose their internal unity and interaction?

A question arises: why did prominent French historians Duby and Le Roy Laduri who began as historians of the peasantry and agrarian relations switched over to the problems of history of culture, mentality, the family and demography? Why did the Russian school of agrarian history of Western Europe (that can boast of the names of Luchitsky, Kareyev, Vinogradov, Kovalevsky, Savin, Petrushevsky, Kosminsky, Neusykhin, Gratsiansky and Skazkin) stop functioning at the turn of the 70s? Why did their pupils turn to the history of culture, social psychology and historical demography? This can hardly be regarded as a mere coincidence explained by a generation change. Each historian is free to choose his subject while historiography as a whole reveals a definite trend—we are witnessing a shift of interests that has many reasons behind it. Here is one, probably the decisive, reason.

Historians of socio-economic relationships feel it necessary to combine this level of reality with others and to discover the links that tied together the European agrarian system of the Middle Ages and New Time and the contemporary demographic structures, socio-psychological and cultural phenomena. They are fully aware that the context of the economic and social processes and phenomena under study should be extended.

Here is what my own experience has taught me (by recurring to one's own experience one avoids the danger of imposing on other historians explanations they would probably decline). While studying the history of the peasantry and the genesis of feudalism in England and Scandinavia in the early Middle Ages I ran into a dead end: I found it impossible to understand how the early feudal social structures appeared when I remained restricted by the traditional range of problems and sources. I felt that the historical material was pushing me towards a more profound analysis of the axiological system and socio-cultural ideas shared by the people who had been creating and reshaping these structures. Far from detracting me from the social structures this analysis led me deeper into them and allowed me to expose their real humanistic content. It was not a departure from socio-economic history—it was a new approach to it. It came to be regarded as global social history that united in a natural way people's social and economic practice and their ideas and thoughts about this practice, the world and man. Far from passively reflecting this practice the mental sphere forms its inalienable part and determines in many respects social behaviour of groups and individuals.

It is interesting to look at the difference between the sources selected by the historians of the agrarian school and by our contemporaries. Our teachers relied on land cadastres, acts of gifts and other legal and economic documents that registered the relationships of landownership and land tenure, the content of rents and peasant duties, notes on the common law and government acts. It is much more difficult to enumerate the sources used by the historians of the new trend: they naturally use the traditional sources and include into their scope narrations (chronicles and hagiography), poetry and epics, sagas and sermons and other literary genres. Specialists in historical demography have turned their attention to parish registers and wills, that is, mass, or serial, sources that can be computerised.

Additional information about the social and economic systems is not an aim in itself—the historians aim at the human dimension. To quote Marc Bloch, a historian is not unlike an ogre in fairy tales: "Where there is human spirit, there is his reward". Can the words "human dimension" be expressed in stricter terms?

Our predecessors mainly relied on objective observation and analysis as the methods of source studies. They used them to disclose the material structure and scrutinised them as if from outside. A historian felt himself a natural scientist in relations to people and structures. This is a necessary and inevitable method naturally used by historians throughout the world.

Is this method sufficient?

One should not confuse humanitarian knowledge aimed at disclosing the meaning and the natural scientific knowledge aimed at disclosing laws of nature. Any historian studies people who lived long or not so long before him: he is engaged in a constant dialogue with them and ask them (or rather historical sources they created) the questions that interest him as our contemporary. He makes his best to hear and understand their answers. This inevitably leads to a conclusion that history cannot be studied with the methods of outside descriptions alone. While identifying social and economic structures it is important to identify the point of view of those who formed these structures—their attitude to the world and emotional and intellectual reactions to it.

At all times people have their specific idea of the world and behave more in accordance with the imaginary picture of the world rather than outside circumstances. Here by imaginary I mean not so much clear and arranged systems of thinking but the entire pool of vague and spontaneous reactions of the human mind, the entire imaginary world. To a great degree human behaviour and values are determined by his language, religion, education and the people around him. One can easily conceive a man devoid of an ideology that would determine his stance in life but it is impossible to conceive a human being that lacks mentality—it greatly determines his social behaviour.

I would not go into greater details here[13] though I want to emphasise that the method of objective studies of the social and economic structures and their development should be complemented with the method of probing deep inside the historical process and the positions of its participants. One cannot avoid attempts to penetrate their historically determined actions and the behavioural models determined by the objective material life and people's world perception and vision of the world.

The picture of the world that is culturally determined is an enormous and objective force that channels the course of history. One should renounce an erroneous point of view that has become deeply embedded in our minds telling that the ideas and intellectual attitudes are not more than ripples on the surface of history unable to change its course. It goes without saying that one should be able to distinguish between the time-serving fluctuations in public moods and the deeply rooted behavioural models. The latter are rooted in the axiological systems inherited from the past. Such automatic responses of the mind that are barely recognised cannot be explicitly formulated—they can be outlined mainly through the studies of individual or group behaviour. They are enormously stable and can reproduce themselves. Their stability is great because these non-personal determinants of an individual are not totally recognised by him and cannot be critically assessed.

If a researcher is not inclined to take them into account or does not know how to do this he fails to produce a profound explanation of the process of history. Reluctance or inability to take such "subjective factors" into account boomerang on politicians—we have seen this more than once.

To repeat: the method of "objective, or outside" study of society should be combined with the method of its studies from "inside", from the point of view of society's members. The principles of their combination cannot be formulated beforehand—everything depends on the aims of the present research. One thing is clear—these methods should be combined and the "inside" opinion is essential for our understanding of any structure formed by people. Historians employ this "internal" position to demonstrate the illusions and false consciousness of any age or period. At the same time this false consciousness does not lose its effectiveness as an active component of the process of history.

Studies of the historical process' subjective side bring to light human activity, individual and group wills and the mechanisms of the transformations of their real interests into the motive forces as people themselves think them to be. Very often these motive forces are far from class or other material interests—they are born by the ideal models created in their minds by culture, religion and traditions of all kinds. Do we have the right to ignore or underestimate the "margin of freedom,, invariably present in human society? Life allows many behavioural variants including "irrational" or seemingly irrational ones.

Experience has shown that all numerous attempts to single out the material and economic factors out of the heterogeneous and contradictory complex of human motives result in an oversimplified, poor and black-and-white picture of history.

Evidently, this is far removed from any attempts a la Diltey to blend with another age and to feel at home in it. Such procedures defy scientific verification, they are subjective and suit more authors of historical fiction rather than a serious researcher who is studying the past on the firm foundation of objective scientific procedures. Historian has no right to abandon his position of an outside observer of a social and intellectual universum and people's world outlook and behaviour.

To illustrate. Studies of the credit and usurer activity in the Middle Ages and the Renaissance are indispensable for an understanding of monetary circulation and the prerequisites of early capitalism as parts of social history. However, profound knowledge of the structure of monetary credit and the sizes of bankers' capitals or specific features of Italian bookkeeping is not enough. The historian cannot escape the questions of the role of money and usurers between the 13th and 16th centuries as seen by the Church and the bankers' and usurers' moral status. Religion and the social-psychological climate in town and countryside determined the ethical norms in economy. These postulates that were seemingly very far from the material side of life affected the bankers' and usurers' practice to the greatest degree. They urged them to be careful in business matters and not to forget God, the Church and society. Not infrequently, they renounced their rights to pass their money to descendants being apprehensive of punishment for iniquitous wealth and gave them away to charities. The moral religious situation was not alone responsible for the unfavourable conditions of monetary transactions: money-lending was not popular among the urban and rural dwellers and mass social action. I am not going into details of the changes in the moral and political climate in Europe at the beginning of New Time. I shall limit myself to reminding the reader of the ties that existed between the reformist and other trends, on the one hand, and the new ethics of entrepreneurship that sanctioned monetary transactions, on the other. In his *Protestant Ethic* and the *Spirit of Capitalism* Max Weber discussed this problem. The specific nature of his suppositions notwithstanding, the methodology of studies of religious and ethical teachings as a component part of important socio-economic processes suggested by the German sociologist and historian is useful.

Weber approached these problems from the positions of historical sociology that he was developing. There are other socio-psychological approaches that embraced an individual's entire picture of the world—irrespective of the period or a class or social group he belongs to. It looks at a broad range of world perception: from his attitude to nature to the way he feels the course of time and history; from the image of death and the other world to his assessment of childhood, old age, women, marriage and the family; from people's emotional sphere to their attitude to labour, wealth, poverty and property. Human personality, the way society assesses it and its self-consciousness and self-assessment forms the pivot of the picture of the world. I believe that precisely the problem of personality and individuality and the degree to which an individual is incorporated into a social group (or social groups) or is completely free of them is the linchpin on which the studies of the picture of the world of any period hinges.

Until recently social historians were riveted to social structures, large groups and classes. As a rule they ignored an individual as an atom of society. Is profound and complete knowledge of the whole possible without similarly complete and profound knowledge of its component parts? Historical knowledge as a dialogue between contemporary man and an individual of the past rests on the knowledge of the latter. This dawned on us but recently—everyone is concerned with a better knowledge of man. Psychologists and philosophers, natural scientists and writers are engaged in discussions of man. Historians are no exception. This is not merely the latest fashion. Time has come for history to recover its status of a humanitarian discipline concerned with man. Only by concentrating on the history of people can history grasp its genuine subject of research. It should proceed not only from outside but also from the inside. History always regards man as a member of a group or society; it is not interested in an abstract man—it concentrates on a historically specific participant in a social process.

For my part, I am somewhat uneasy about the calls to study man heard from all sides—I would rather see this key concept of social history and historical sociology relieved from its fashionable aura which sometimes pushes its genuine content to the background. I am not inclined to regard the general philosophical deliberations "on the role of human subjectivity in history" divorced from the specific experience of historians as unproductive.[14] Historiography, including Russian historiography, has traditions of its own—here I have in mind B. Romanov's book about man in Old Russials[15] and D. Likhachev's monograph about Old Russian literature and an individual in it.[16] This shows that historians, and historians of culture, have long embarked on the road leading to human history and away from depersonalised history. These attempts should rest on a firm methodological foundation.

Insistent calls for interdisciplinary approaches are closely connected with the problem of man in history; historians can engage its neighbours—literary studies, historical poetics in particular, linguistics and especially semiotics and the history of arts—to conduct in-depth studies of man in history. On the other hand, history is a science sui *generis* that needs not dissolve itself in other disciplines. There is a need, however, to learn from other sciences and look more closely at their methods and the way they formulate questions. New knowledge may come from a new way of posing questions to the already studied historical sources or posing them more insistently. We should not ignore wider vistas opened up by the cultural and socio-anthropological approaches to history.

This will provide a clearer picture of both internally connected hypostases of social history—social structures and people that were part of them. Social history is concerned with people united into groups.

This approach presupposes penetration into the sphere of culture present in all structures and individuals. Society is dead outside it. It is totally clear that by culture I do not mean a sum total of achievements of the human spirit, the traditional subject that has outlived itself in *Kulturgeschichte* or autonomous *Geistesgeschichte.* Within social history culture is a system of man's orientations in life and the real content of individual minds. An individual joins together the social and cultural elements in himself and they shape him. One is unable to understand social development while ignoring the personality structure pertaining to this social system—in the same way the system and people that form it cannot be grasped out of their truly human nature, this is, culture.

Eric Hobsbawn, a prominent British historian, wrote in his time that we should switch from social history to history of society.[17] I tend to agree with him provided the history of society is placed within its cultural content, that is, the human content of the social elements.

We are witnessing a powerful expansion of social history outside its traditional framework. Is this expansion fraught with the danger of it being dissolved in an indefinite global history and of it losing the specific subject of study? Opposite is true—social history is now looking for a subject-matter of its own. Only an eclectic approach that fails to identify the main and decisive things can deprive social history of its identity. The current search will enrich social history, rather than impoverish it by taking away its subject-matter.

Here is an example of enrichment that occurred on the borderline between the social and the cultural—a distinction between the official, or learned, culture on the one hand, and folk, or unofficial, culture, on the other that has been introduced into history. The definition of "folk culture" is far from accurate and invites heated debates. (It is not my task here to go into details—I have already written about this elsewhere.) The problem itself is very important and cannot but raise doubts. We are called upon to abandon the traditions of studying the history of culture as the elite's exceptional possession and the result of its activity. The models thus obtained are popularised and vulgarised in the broader sections of society that passively accumulate them. We are called upon to study the mode of thought and feeling of rank-and-file members of society, to reveal to the world a different approach to man and reality that was typical of the toiling people who belonged to the lower strata of propertied classes and to have-nots. This world perception was an inalienable part of their social practice therefore their conduct and the soil that produced unique and elegant cultural creations cannot be understood without a close analysis of culture's lower layer that was poorly and inaccurately formulated.

This approach is employed in folklore studies. Still, prior to the 60s, before Mikhail Bakhtin put forward his conception of the folk carnival culture and French historians clearly formulated the question of an opposition and mutual influence of the culture of the elite and the culture and religious feelings of the common people this problem has not received an equally close attention. A new continent—"culture of the silent majority", of the wide sections that were divorced from books and were unable to register their ideas, strivings and sentiments in a written form[18] —is looming in front of specialists in the Middle Ages and New Time. It is to be explored in greater detail. The history and theory of small groups can hardly produce good results unless more attention is paid to the ideas, socio-cultural constructs, beliefs and customs, habitual stereotypes of thought and behaviour that moved individual members of these groups.

While working on the history of the lowest cultural strata we are extending their ideas on social structures as a living organism brimming with human content.

Social history of the end of the 20th century could not but turn into socio-cultural history.

NOTES

[1] D. Kovalchenko, Methods of Historical Research, Moscow, 1987 (in Russian).

[2] J Topolski, *Metodologia historii,* Warsaw, 1968; idem., *Teoria wiedzy historycznej,* Poznan, 1983; *Miedzy historia a teoria. Refleksje nd problematyka dziejom i wiedzy historycznej.* Red. M. Drozdowskiego, Warsaw Poznan, 1988.

[3] E. M. Staerman, "On the Problem of Emergence of State in Rome", *Vestnik drevnei istorii,* 1988, No. 2; V. I. Kuzishchin, E. M. Staerman, "Problems of the Class Structure and Class Struggle in Contemporary Historiography", *Voprosy istorii* 1986, No. 10.

[4] A. Ya. Gurevich, *Problems of Genesis of Feudalism in Western Europe,* Moscow, 1970 (in Russian).

[5] J. Duby, Les trois ordres ou l'imaginaire du feodalisme, Paris, 1987; J. Le Goff, "Les trois fonctions indoeuropeennes: L'historien et l'Europe feodale," *Annales.* E.S.C., 34, 1979, No. 6.

[6] O, A. Dobiash-Rozhdestvenskaya, *Church Society in France in the 13th Century,* Part I, *Parish,* Petrograd, 1914 (in Russian).

[7] E. Le Roy Ladurie, *Montaillou, village occitan de 1294 d 1324,* Paris, 1975.

[8] A. Ya. Gurevich, *The Problems of the Genesis of Feudalism...,* p. 63 ff., speaking at the colloqium of Soviet and American historians (Moscow, October 1989) N. Zemon-Davis spoke about an exchange of gifts in New Time.

[9] C. Ginzburg, C. Poni, "La micro-histoire", *Le debat,* No. 17,1981, pp. 133-136.

[10] G. M. Trevelyan, *English Social History,* London, 1942.

[11] F. Braudel, *Civilisation mate'rielle, economie et capitalisme, xv-xvn siecle.* Vol. I, *Les structures de quotidien: Le possible et l'impossible,* Paris, 1979. Vol II. *Les jeux de l'echange,* Paris, 1979.

[12] M. Bloch, L'Apologie pour l'histoire, Paris, 1959.

[13] Gurevich A. Ya, "Historical Science and Historical Anthropology", *Voprosy* filoso~i, 1988, No. 1, pp. 56-70; idem., "Historical Anthropology: Problems of Social and Cultural History", *Herald of the USSR Academy of Sciences,,* 1989, No. 7, pp. 71-78 (in Russian).

[14] M. A. Barg, "On the Role of Human Subjectivity in History", *Istoria SSSR,* 1989, No. 3, pp. 115-131.

[15] B. A. Romanov, *People and Customs in Old Russia,* Leningrad, 1947 (in Russian).

[16] D. S. Likhachev, *Man in Old Russian Literature,* Moscow, 1976; idem, *Poetics of Old Russian Literature,* Leningrad, 1967 (both in Russian).

[17] E. J. Hobsbawn, "From Social History to the History of Society", *Daedalus,* Vol. 199, 1971, No. 1, pp. 20-45.

[18] A. Ya. Gurevich, *Mediaeval World: Culture of the Silent Majority,* Moscow, 1990 (in Russian).

MODELLING THE HISTORICAL PROCESS

Grigori Pomerants[*]

In varying scales of time and space, the human imagination uncovers, with a greater or lesser degree of accuracy, those accumulative wave-like or explosive processes that interact in history.

When an idea begins to take shape one can always find predecessors. The same happened when I began to formulate this article. When looking through Dietmar Rothermund's article,[1] I found that my own predecessors were Immanuel Kant[2] and Friedrich von Schlegel. Kant was the first to show that whether any pattern or rationale can be found in history depends to a considerable extent on the scale applied. If the scale is small then accidental occurrences will be most evident. If the scale is large then the accumulative processes become obvious and one can point out the tendency towards universal political unification (world government).

Schlegel sharply criticized this conception. He drew on the experience of India, which then was first capturing the imagination of Europeans, to create a romantic model of history as a series of independent localised processes. In his view, all the great cultures were equal in value. Each underwent the same evolution, beginning with a mystical revelation out of which that culture's basic values first arose and then proceeding towards rational, sterile constructions. The end was a superficially educated society that had lost its creative impulse .

Today, 200 years after Kant, we may note that the West has indeed progressed towards the League of Nations and then the United Nations, to the EEC and NATO, and to the idea of a world government. The logic of Chinese and Indian development, however, has certainly not led towards the same end.

[*] **G. Pomerants**, historian snd philologist, specialises in culturology philosophy and the history of literature. Author of some articles on these themes in *Transactions of Tartu University,* in collections of articles *Ideological Trends of Modern India, Theoretical Problems of Studying Literatures of the Far East and others,* as well as of books published in the FRG, France and the USA.

Local differences disappeared from the Kantian model of linear evolution. Non-European cultures could only be included as junior partners and variants of the ancient or mediaeval stages of development through which Europe had already passed. In Schlegel's model, on the contrary, it was the unity of the historical process that disappeared. His conception did not permit any worldwide and unified measure of historical time.

Both models are actually older than Kant and Schlegel. In classical times St Augustine promoted the idea of the unity of history: he rejected cyclical conceptions in favour of the uniqueness of Christ's birth ("the one and only son of God") and of his resurrection from the dead. The sources of this linear conception go back even further, to the promised coming of the Jewish Messiah. However, the Bible also says that "to everything there is a season" (Ecclesiastes). In the historiography of the Ancient Greeks, Indians and Chinese the cyclical conception of history predominates. There is also, however, linear movement not only upwards (to the coming of the Messiah, the Second Coming of Christ, and into the radiant future) but also downwards, from the Golden to the Iron Age. Thus an eternal repetition and accumulative development in a single direction (even towards decline) has been contemplated over a period of one thousand years.

The new contribution of Kant was his discovery of the historian's viewpoint: from far away the patterns may be discerned, while from close to only chaos seems to reign. Schlegel did not refute this discovery—he was also demonstrating the existence of larger patterns. However, for him these patterns were not necessarily linear and accumulative, and certainly not indisputably "progressive". Decadence might also increase, for instance. A patterned and regular development might move like a pendulum swinging or unfold in cyclical, spiral, etc., forms. The total historical motion is internally complex and can be analytically divided into many other motions; when a certain scale in the division of historical time and space is applied each of these component motions becomes clearly visible. I am inclined to distinguish, at the least, four to five scales of space, and as many time-scales. We may restrict ourselves to our immediate surroundings (the walls of Rome or Athens, for instance); to a country or empire; to the boundaries of a cultural world (Islam, Christendom); to a system made up of two interacting worlds (the East and Western Mediterranean); or, finally, the entire world. In the temporal dimension a day may suffice, or we may write the chronicles of reigns and dynasties, and think in terms of entire historical epochs and archaeological periods (Palaeolithic, Neolithic, Bronze Age). Finally, we may divide all that is historical into the infinite cosmic waves of *pravritti* (unfolding of existing, evolution) and *nivritti* (rolling up, or involution).

First we shall discard the Indian concepts of *mahayuga* and *mahacalpa* which apply to a scale too vast for our purposes. Those that remain we shall divide into four points of view. Let us begin with the largest scale: in spatial terms this means the entire planet, while in temporal terms we are thinking of tens of thousands of years for the Stone Age and several thousand years during which there is written history. At this level the problems of blind alleys and zigzags in development disappear of their own accord. The civilisations of pre-Columbian America do not fit into the pattern since they are too unstable and, on this scale, petty and inconspicuous. The Middle Ages only occupy one millimetre, figuratively speaking, and we can pass directly from Archimedes to Galileo. This scale is most convenient for examining the history of prehistoric society. We know only of scattered points which are separated by tens of thousands of years. If we join them with a line a picture of progressive change, the emergence of *Homo sapiens,* almost naturally arises. There are blind alleys and failures but they do not change the overall picture. We ourselves are seen as the goal of development and the progressing or accumulative coincides with the progressive or good. Still not having reached the lowest threshold of romanticism, there is no argument that development here is a gain not a loss. The most ardent romantics, in as far as I can remember, do not wish to again become apes, pithecanthropoids or at least Neanderthal men and women. They wish to remain rational human beings and therefore the accumulative changes that led to the emergence of rational man are regarded by all scholars with much the same feelings. They unanimously all consider blind alleys and regressive lines to be precisely that, blind alleys and regressive lines. There is no romantic yearning for hairy paws and protuberant brows.

Continuing our reflections in this vein, we may note the ladder-like ascent of those accumulative progressive shifts which we term revolutions. First, the adoption of tools, by making axes and scrapers from stone flakes of a particular form. Second, the pictorial revolution of the late Palaeolithic when the first images were made and man first thought of the "object in general" as opposed to the object in its specific everyday context. Third, came the agricultural or late Neolithic revolution. Fourth, the intellectual revolution of the "axial time" in the 1st millennium B. C. when individual ways of thinking guided by logic arose in place of those based on folklore and mythology. Finally, there came the industrial, scientific and technical revolutions of the modern period.

However, from the third item in our list onwards disputes arise as to whether all these shifts were progressive or not. As soon as man begins to leave traces of his aesthetic and spiritual activities, e.g. the first cliff drawings, doubts are cast. Toynbee lamented the victory of the Neolithic craftsman over the Palaeolithic artist. We must admit that only the total lack of information about the intellectual, moral and aesthetic life of Neanderthal men allows us to claim their progress was indisputable. As soon as we begin to examine these accumulative shifts in a wide scope they are revealed as being functional and beneficial in some senses and dysfunctional in others, creating difficulties and even capable of destroying humanity.

Now let us turn to the medium global and planetary level or scale. The Earth, as before, remains our spatial dimension but now we take a century or two as our unit of time. This wide spatial scope ensures that we do not pay attention to local cultures that have been side-tracked in blind alleys and perished there. We focus on the cultures of oecumen or distinct areas of human habitation[3] that have existed continuously throughout written history. These are China and India with their surrounding respective daughter civilisations, and the Near East and the West. (As we have already remarked, the latter two together form a single bi-(sub)oecumen, the Mediterranean.) As we observe their history we come up against the problem of the "Middle Ages" (a reaction to the intellectual leap of the axial time) and note a pendular swing. The archaic period, classical times, Middle Ages and the modern era combine to form a kind of succession and decorative border: the feminine, more holistic than partial (and in this sense "dark") *yin* ages are succeeded by the masculine *yang* epochs which are directed towards discovery of man and the world as rationally conceivable objects (and in this sense an "enlightened" age). This succession may be observed in all oecumen, though it is less clear in China and India than in the Mediterranean. Everywhere archaic thought is stronger in its understanding of the whole than of its parts. For this reason the mytho-poetic and early philosophical constructs of this period remain unsurpassed as models of the unity of culture (they include the Upanishads, the first Daoist works and pre-Socratic writings). At the same time, they are obscure in particulars, logically imperfect or quite alogical. Classic thought everywhere distinguishes logic as a particular discipline (or philosophical school that emphasises logical investigation) and perfects the analysis of particularities, but to some extent loses its feeling for the whole. The demythologisation of culture reduces it to a lower level: the wise men are replaced by the sophists and the superficial education of which Schlegel complained becomes predominant. Yet this is far from being the end of civilisation, as he supposed. In all these subhabitats history turned this full stop into a comma. Early mediaeval culture arose from the crisis caused by the intellectualism of the axial period. Drawing on certain traditions of the archaic period which had stood the test of time (in some cases, these traditions were borrowed—the Jewish tradition in the West, that of India in China), this culture created a new integral system. In new embodiments the logical and mythological approaches gained a new unity. A new common language of symbols was formed uniting the educated upper strata of society with the ignorant lower estates which remained at an archaic and pre-archaic, primitive level.

The development of China, India and the Near East in this way achieved stability and such oscillations as there were took place within one and the same system. In the West, however, the synthesis proved unstable. From repeated crises there emerged the Modern Period which led to our present, global scientific and technological civilisation. The crisis in this new civilisation is the first to embrace the whole planet in history: its collapse could be universal and it is hard to imagine any solution from without, like the incursion of barbarian hordes.

We may term the third scale, medium-local. In spatial terms we take a local culture, and in time, a century or less (Ancient Egyptian culture may be measured in centuries, for example, while contemporary culture in decades). At this level we are most struck by the blind alleys in evolution. There are very few stable civilisations that successfully emerge from crises. These are the sub-oecumen and, perhaps, a few more cultural foci within those sub-oecumen. All remaining civilisations were unstable and perished. The continuity between them was very weak and sometimes absent altogether. How were the empires of Attila and Genghis Khan, which were separated by many centuries and both came into being and disintegrated in the same steppes, linked one to another? Even agricultural civilisations, though they ploughed the same land, more often inherited tools and ways of working from each other than those distinctive features which constituted their individual character. When the Hebrews reached Hanaan, the Promised Land, they learnt to till the soil but did not adopt the deities of its pagan inhabitants. The modern Egyptian fellahin are in some sense the descendants of the peasants of Ancient Egypt. Yet they speak Arabic and consider themselves Arabs and Muslims. Egypt of the Pharaohs disappeared and all that remained were the temples and pyramids.

If we are to return from historic pessimism to a moderate optimism we must go back to the second level or scale. Then we shall be able to agree with the later Toynbee: civilisations live and die so that humanity can take the next step in its spiritual development. The cycle of birth, growth and death in local civilisations is comparable to the spinning of circular saw which cuts deeper into the trunk with each revolution... The possibility that history and the historical process have a meaning is preserved—but only if we identify ourselves with a "world" (universal) religion which embraces an oecumen at least, and not with a local culture.

The fourth scale could be called anthropomorphic. In terms of space it is the human experience of events. These events thrash about like microbes in a drop of dirty water. Certain of them grow and leave traces in world history. Yet they do not thereby acquire a perceptible meaning: the underlying pattern is too faint. Raids by the nomads of the steppes on Russian towns and villages, for instance, occurred every now and again and were always possible. There is no reason, however, that can explain the extent of the Mongol conquests, apart from those tied up with the personality of Genghis Khan. The poet Daniil Andreyev metaphorically claimed that Temuchin was a medium who became the "human weapon" of powerful demons. This explanation merely transfers the irrationality to another, this time demonic level. If Timuchin had not become Genghis Khan then the Mongols would have been unlikely to reach the battlefield of Kalka and, as a consequence, modern Russia would not have taken the form it did. The East Slavs would probably have evolved a different political system, possibly made up of several different countries, and they would have possessed different characters.

"History is a realm in which human freedom and natural necessity are curiously mingled," wrote Reinhold Niebuhr. "Man's freedom constantly creates the most curious and unexpected and unpredictable emergences and emergencies in history. All efforts to discern patterns of recurrence, after the manner of Spengler and Toynbee, or patterns of development, in the fashion of Hegel, Spencer or Comte, must do violence to the infinite variety in the strange configurations of history."[4]

The difference between the optimistic conceptions of linear development and the pessimistic conceptions of eternal recurrence cease to be of substance, in Niebuhr's view. Any linking together of facts at the level of the large- or medium-scale is regarded, from the anthropomorphic level, as violence against reality. Such a viewpoint carries great weight in those absurd situations when historical patterns cannot be discerned or if they can, do not offer any comfort.

Sometimes the anthropomorphic scale is complemented and reinforced by the theomorphic (which in our terms is the most specific or zero scale). God's viewpoint is introduced, in which the unit of time is infinity. Infinity and time cannot be logically coordinated. Nevertheless, the eternal is introduced into history as Providence which strives towards its own undeclared goal; or it is expressed as the game *(lila)* of Brahman, Vishnu or Shiva that has no goal and is sufficient in itself. The theomorphic scale allows us to locate its values in the Heavens, above the meaningless whims of fate, and thus give human life (which has no historical meaning) a certain spiritual meaning. The anthropomorphic and theomorphic scales form a well-balanced unity. The Enlightenment when it destroyed the theomorphic scale created the necessity of the idea of progress as compensation. The crisis of faith in progress then removed this comfort. Only the anthropomorphic scale remained, which without the theomorphic was in itself absurd. Albert Camus used the ancient myth of Sisyphus to express the spirit of this situation.

Let us now look more closely at certain problems that arise when shifting between viewpoints of different scale. We begin with the first level. Here we can identify several parallel and accumulative processes: the rationalisation of human relations with nature; the growth of the forces of production; increase on the division of labour; the differentiation of culture into separate fields; the differentiation of society into separate strata; the enlargement of the units of social integration (from lineage to tribe to nation, etc). Taken together these processes may be termed movement towards the noosphere, as Vernadsky and Teilhard de Chardin termed it, i.e. towards a certain hypothetical condition in which humanity attains maturity. Or, if one holds a pessimistic view of development, it represents a movement towards global catastrophe and disintegration.

Marx considered that growth of the forces of production was the most important of these processes, and determining all the others. Yet the forces of production amount to no more than instruments the object of labour and labour power. The objects of labour develop very slowly by themselves (a bog may be drained, for instance, but a meadow also becomes marshy). Instruments of labour do not develop at all without human willpower. The development of the forces of production therefore amounts to no more than the evolution of labour power. To regard man as labour power, though, is to arbitrarily select only one aspect of the whole: for men and women act, reflect, play, think, pray, dance and so on. The primacy of the forces of production is only singled out because man's working activities are thought to be historically the most important. According to the theory, those upheavals that do not affect the economy have less influence on the course of history than a new "means of production". If we start from Marx's viewpoint then we shall see that he does not say that everything new begins in the economic sphere. It may instead arise out of a carefree play (domestication of animals), abstract thought (many inventions), religious quests (the movements which contributed much to the genesis of capitalism) and so on. Moreover, for Marx the realm of necessity was a prelude, it was prehistory: within it constantly accumulated the elements of freedom that would eventually permit the transition from prehistory to history. Hence the attention which all Marxists devoted to such non-economic forms of activity as the development of consciousness, of the revolutionary movement, etc. Marx himself did not at all consider that the decisive role of economic activities was a constant and eternal law of history. In the future, he believed, it would be abolished by the leap from the realm of necessity to that of freedom.[5] Today it is obvious that the economy did not always resolve all issues in the past either. Up to a certain period, perhaps until the beginning of the Modern Era itself, the economy as an independent sphere of social existence could not be observed.

In tribal societies economic activities are inseparable from religious rituals while in the empires of archaic times they form part of the administrative responsibilities. It is impossible to talk of the primacy of that which has no independent existence and thus we cannot speak of the primacy of economics before a certain historical period without committing a logical error. Another formulation of Marx appears much more fruitful: all historical epochs can be viewed as epochs in the progressive division of labour.[6] If we expand this thesis a little we may derive from it the basic conception of the French sociologist Emile Durkheim and his school (which took shape after Marx and, perhaps, under his influence). It is extremely convenient to see the differentiation of human activities as the leitmotiv of the historical process. It is uninterrupted on the large scale, and all the remaining accumulative processes are linked to it.

This does not mean that the development of instruments of labour loses its importance in denoting a certain stage of development. In certain cases, we simply do not possess any forms of historical evidence other than axes, scrapers, etc. It was not Marx but his archaeologist predecessors who thought up the terms "stone age", "bronze age", and "iron age". There were also repeated attempts to take this labelling further, "in our age, the age of steamships and railroads", etc. Marx's conception is simply the most convincing of such attempts. An elegant system, it enables us to look at all of "prehistory" (in his terms) from the Old Stone Age to the present from a single point of view. However, from the moment that historians had more sources at their disposal—even beginning with the cliff drawings of the Upper Palaeolithic, and certainly when written records begin to appear—it became possible to investigate several constants at the same time, not just economic but also spiritual, political, religious and other elements.

The problem remains of the coordination of these variables and deciding which of them is central. It turns out that the most obvious candidate, material culture, does not fit this role although it is so convenient for distinguishing the first stages in the historical process. Attempts, as Marx himself put it, to deduce the structure of the Oriental heavens from the lack of private property in land[7] do not lead to any convincing conclusion. Not to mention the banality of the commonplace results of a sociological analysis of literature and so on.

The degree of differentiation or another definition of the system as a whole is an extremely convenient basis for development. Then we do not need to deduce the state of certain spheres from that of others (an exercise that in any case does not always work, stagnation in one field being at times accompanied by strenuous development in another). Instead we see each sphere in the context of the entire social structure of which it forms a part: it is the nature of that framework which now seems "primary" and not what happens within it. It becomes by no means obligatory for the development of the parts to precede that of the whole. Usually innovation arises first in a particular sphere from which it comes to influence the entire system. It is also important, however, that the very possibility of this novelty emerging depends on the central variable (on the level of differentiation in the social system, say, or the level of rationality underlying relations and so on). The impulse might flow from politics to religion (first the Roman Empire, then Christianity) or in the reverse direction (first Buddhism, then the empires of Ashoka and Kanishka; first Islam, then the Caliphate). Yet this could only happen after society as a whole had attained a definite condition or level.

It is also important that the state of the system is always immediately obvious beginning with the most primitive forms of society. The Bushmen of Southern Africa are organised in clans, although they have neither a faith nor a system of government or, in other terms, neither politics nor economics. All that exist are certain aspects of a common life in society. Therefore primitive societies can only be studied as a whole, as indeed ethnographers, ethnologists and social anthropologists do. And the possibility to pose the question: what comes first, economy or religion, appears comparatively late.

Finally, even when all these spheres have taken shape and been separated and one can debate as to which of them is more important, the general structural approach retains the convenience that it allows all spheres to be described in the same terms. Moreover, there is a real similarity behind this common terminology.

The model of the primary and secondary goes back to the atomism of Democritus. There is no whole, only atoms and empty space. The billiard cue strikes the ball and it rolls into the pocket. The basis presses on the pedal and the wheels of the superstructure begin to turn. The motion of these balls may be very complicated but unless the cue first strikes them they will not move at all. In these cases, therefore, interaction is subordinated with methodological inevitability to a mechanical causation. It has the same previously determined final cause as the billiard cue or the libido in Freudian psychoanalysis. Marx and Engels protested against the vulgarisation of their ideas but their pupils uncovered the material interests underlying political and spiritual movements with the same relentless consistency as Freudians in pursuit of the Oedipus complex.

The model of history as a growing division of labour presupposes, on the contrary, a unity and its subdivision. (This bears analogy with the Hindu *prakritti* which is divided into three *guna*—aspects or threads—which after a number of subsequent divisions and combinations lead to objects.) The problem of interaction is always in the foreground here while mechanical causation only explains relatively secondary, partial linkages.

In the theory of development the central variable may be any parameter that is clearly expressed at a given time. The main thing is not to lose sight of the wood for the trees; the overall movement proceeds beyond these parameters and not all accumulative processes are beneficial. Some processes may be definitely dysfunctional and destructive while others are beneficial and functional and dysfunctional at the same time. For example, the developing personality in a differentiated society is presented with increasing opportunities that have many negative effects: alienation, a sense of bewilderment and abandonment in a world that is too hostile, complex and incomprehensible. The more differentiated societies, as a rule, are less stable. In such a strongly differentiated society as that in which we now live the threat of disintegration faces us on every side. We have been forced to understand that the forces of production are destructive and may destroy all the biosphere. Now we realise that periodic slowing down or halting of devel-

opment is as essential as leaps forward; we can see that restoration is no less
fruitful than revolution .

We must not look on periods of restoration as unfortunate accidents or
the actions of evil forces opposed to the sacred cause of progress (nor regard the
latter as free of contradictions and leading humanity straight to a radiant future).
Almost any development is both a curse and a benefit. Take, for example, life
itself. The transition from single cell structures to the multicellular means the loss
of the capacity to live forever, with no knowledge of death, like amoebae and in-
fusoria. A threshold arises which the organism cannot transcend and the species
is continued only in its descendants. Death is the price to be paid for complexity
and the possibility of a moral and intellectual life ...

The same is true of the history of human society. Every step forward in
development and differentiation is simultaneously a step to the edge of the abyss
and threatens the loss of stability or disintegration .

Development is thus a sequence in which differentiation is followed by
the restoration of that disrupted unity. This perception leads us to a second view
of history and to the search for the rhythms that guide the alternation between
demythologising and remythologising epochs, classicism and romanticism, and
yin and yang. As already noted, this rhythm is most easily traced at the second
level when we are observing the transition from Antiquity to the Middle Ages,
and from mediaeval times to the Modern Period. Within the Modern Period, however, which we know better than preceding eras, there is also a distinctive
rhythm. Although less pronounced, it is entirely comparable to the former: from
renaissance to baroque, from classicism and enlightenment to sentimentalism and
romanticism, and from naturalism to decadence. It would seem there were similar
shifts in the Middle Ages as well. For exactly this reason it is possible that there
were smaller-scale periods of renaissance before the 15th-century Italian renaissance (Carolingian, Ottonian and that in 12th-century France; those in the Mus-
lim world, Georgia and China). Moreover, these small-scale periods of renaissance may not be inferior to the quattrocento in the importance of their philosophical, literary or artistic attainments. It is in the historical sense that they are
less important: they did not represent a large-scale turning point but remained
within the limits of the Middle Ages.

At the second level, or from the second point of view which cuts through
all levels, history is made up of constant internal contradictions. The basic contradiction of any existence is to remain specific and complete and simultaneously
be both unified and whole and individual and unique. The unity when it becomes
a unique loses its unity; the unique by becoming a unity, loses its uniqueness.
Therefore, the Creator, if we imagine him behind the driving-wheel, must be
constantly steering now to the right and now to the left: otherwise, the vehicle

will not travel straight down the middle of the road. With our delayed perception of time these swings of the wheel appear to be major epochs.

In terms of values, the virtues of truth, good and beauty alternate between unity in an entire sacredness or a secularisation that separates them and makes them independent of one another. Whenever they are separated they lose their profundity. We regard the separation of art from religion as progress and yet value religious music and archaic religious paintings as tremendous achievements.

In the intellectual sphere, the striving towards precision leads to a differentiation of disciplines but this differentiation in turn results in the loss of a total view of things. As scholarship and learning develop (i.e. the knowledge of a particular field of objects and their relations) wisdom disappears. The sage is as rare a phenomenon in the streets of New York as the scholar or scientist in archaic Greece or India. The scholar knows his own field and two or three of those more closely related to it; but the universal man would be wasting his time if he turned to him for advice. When learning and knowledge expand with such rapidity the problem of wisdom becomes inconceivably difficult. The sorcerers of the Bushmen knew EVERYTHING that was known in their culture, and for them there was no contradiction between special fields of knowledge and comprehension of the whole. Both could be retained in the one head. Thomas Aquinas gave thanks to God that he had not come across a single incomprehensible page. In his time this was already rare. In our day it is quite impossible. The social sciences are becoming a magic circle and the keys to its gates are lost. A particular discipline of information science has emerged to help seek out individual scraps of knowledge. Yet it cannot give an overall knowledge.

Whenever society, and the knowledge it has of itself, drastically increases in complexity there have always arisen anti-intellectual movements that oppose books and letters in the name of the spirit, unmediated emotion and the wholeness of life. This is true of our time as well. The first trace left by such a movement in history can be found in the Upanishads and the Taoteking, the second—in late Antiquity and the early Middle Ages. Our epoch is again searching for and re-establishing wisdom in "scholarly lack of knowledge". Moral progress is similarly contradictory. We can more easily refer to progress in the moral tasks we face. There is a minimum of solidarity without which no historical collective could survive. When the borders of social integration are expanded, i.e. the collective grows, then this minimum also grows. It is sufficient for a Bushman to keep in regular contact with 40-50 other human beings in whose company he wanders through the desert. This is easy and an average Bushman is a good Bushman. In most tribes it is more difficult to attain solidarity. Therefore the role of external regulation, norms, laws and rules increases. We should not imagine that only the ancient Hebrews were law-givers. The Gogo tribe in Tanzania lays down rules for things that neither Moses nor Ezra would ever have thought of regulating, for example: a man should lie on his right side and caress his wife with his left hand; women should cast out dirty water only to the west; and so on.

The early empires mingled different tribes and tribal laws also became intermingled. The Roman emperors tried to surmount this moral chaos by offering themselves as gods to these different ethnic groups, and treating their decrees as holy writ. Even when they greatly desired to act as a moral example, however, and were themselves capable of doing so, e.g. Marcus Aurelius, their daily duties prevented them. Only Jesus, the son of a carpenter from Nazareth, proved able to succeed where Caesar had failed. He returned to the moral intuition that the lawmakers had neglected and from some depths we have still not fathomed he uncovered in himself a love of each person as though it had been his own child. The Son of God was a genius of humanity who proved capable of loving all the 10, 20 or 30 million subjects of the Roman Empire and the surrounding barbarians, both enemies and friends, as himself. This was the key to the transformation of the faceless masses held in thrall by the Roman laws into a people who were united not only by fear but also by love.

The moral demands and expectations of this new historical entity were higher. Yet it was less successful in some respects than the previous clans and tribes. For instance, it would never occur to a Bushman that it was wrong to kill his enemy and even Moses would have considered this a strange and immoral idea. Yet the overwhelming majority of Christians, "new Adams", could not attain this ideal. The Bushmen were quite faithful and true to both the letter and spirit of their law (indeed, they simply did not distinguish the letter from the spirit). The Old Testament Adams would observe, at the least, the letter of their commandment. The "new Adams" were true to neither the letter nor the spirit of Christianity—or, for that matter, of other advanced doctrines such as Buddhism and the Bhagavat-gita.

If we take a sufficiently large scale we may speak of the irresistible progress in the moral tasks which men and women were set and of which they were conscious. Simultaneously, we should admit, there is also a growing gap between these tasks and human behaviour. The norm or icon becomes more and more refined while the average individual falls further and further below this standard. The barbarians were astounded by the treacherousness of the Byzantines because it was not the deceiver Hermes who was revered in Constantinople but Christ. While the Byzantines prayed to Christ they crucified him again each day (to use a Homiletic metaphor). This is actually the ethical meaning of the crucifixion: Christ on the cross is a symbol of the ethical principles of civilisation and its everyday life.

This might be called the relative moral impoverishment of civilisation as it develops and its moral tasks grow. A certain level of impoverishment is tolerable and compensated by various institutions that take the place of moral solidarity. There is, however, some elusive boundary beyond which Sodom and Gomorrah perish, and the kingdom of Ashurbanipal and Tsin Shihuan, Hitler and Mussolini all die. Human society cannot make do with the institutions and stereotypes that are the product of propaganda: it must have some minimum of natural solidarity born from within.

When we descend to the third level it is the explosive and "irrational" processes that come particularly to the fore, from the birth of the Caliphate to the raids of Genghis Khan and Tamerlane. These specific problems require separate study, however.

NOTES

[1] D. Rothermund, "Geschichtswissenschaft und Entwicklungspolitik", *Vierteljahrshefte fur Zeitgeschichte,* Issue 15, Stuttgart, 1967, Vol. 4, pp. 325-340.

[2] I. Kant, "Idee zur einer allgemeinen Geschichte im Weltburgerlichen Absicht (1784)", 1. *Kant, Die drei Kritihen,* Stuttgart, 1949, p. 460 ff.

[3] G. S. Pomerants, "The Theory of the Sub-Oecumen and the Problem of the Distinctive Nature of Oriental Cultures", *Learned Transactions of Tartu University,* Issue 392, Tartu, 1976, pp. 42-67; idem, "Shenshi as a Type of Mediaeval Scholar", *The History and Culture of China,* Moscow, 1974, pp. 362-384 (both in Russian).

[4] R. Niebuhr, *The Structure of Nations and Empires,* New York, 1959, p. 7.

[5] K. Marx, *Capital, Vol.* 3, Moscow, 1971, pp. 818-820.

[6] K. Marx and F. Engels, *The Cerman Ideology,* Moscow, 1968, pp. 43-46 and 61 ff.

[7] K. Marx and F. Engels, *Selected Correspondence,* Moscow, 1955, p. 99.

GORKY, KOROLENKO AND PAVLOV: IN DIALOGUE WITH THE NEW REGIME

Lev Anninsky[*]

In the years from 1917 to 1921, we have always been told, Gorky was often wrong. Even Soviet schoolchildren know this from hearsay, not to mention adults who take a serious interest in the writer's biography. It is no secret that these mistakes were chiefly to be found in the articles that later made up his book, *Untimely Thoughts*. They were first published in the newspaper *Novaya zhizn* (New Life). Any Soviet encyclopedia today will tell us that this publication was started in April 1917 and was closed in July 1918. In order to preserve Gorky's image as the classic proletarian author such sources prefer not to tell us that it was Gorky who founded and edited the paper. Yet all this is no real secret either and can easily be found out. It was what Gorky actually wrote there which has remained a secret for Soviet readers: we were only told that he had "exaggerated the difficulties and underplayed the achievements of the revolution, giving a subjective interpretation and thereby objectively siding with its opponents, providing ammunition for the enemies of the Soviet state—he could not see the wood for the trees..." In the end Gorky, on the advice of his friends, left the country. He went abroad for medical treatment and observed the revolution from afar: perhaps then he began to see the wood and not just the trees? Gorky went to live in Italy and his mistakes became part of history.

These mistakes have since been described in a moderate tone by Soviet critics, sometimes objectively and in great detail. In other words, there was sorrow and understanding but no fury or ill-will. Yet until 1988 ordinary Soviet

[*] **L. Anninsky,** *literary* critic. author of the books *The 1930s-the 1970S. Essays on Literary Criticism; Lev Tolstoi and the Cinema.* and *Leskov's Necklace,* as well as essays on modern literature.

readers still did not see the offending articles themselves. Quotations from them were very rare and brief.

Even recently our serious authors publicly quote the "misguided" Gorky of those years with extreme caution and the statements he made then were accompanied with a great many explanations. For example, when L. Reznikov wrote his article "On Maxim Gorky's book *Untimely Thoughts" (Neva,* No 1, 1988) he quoted only 200 lines from the book—and each, moreover, was provided with 15 lines of Reznikov's own commentary. When A. Ovcharenko wrote in *Literaturnaya gazeta* (September 14, 1988) it was already known that Gorky's *Untimely Thoughts* would be published in the monthly *Literaturnoe obozrenie:* he quoted more boldly but still gave 4 or 5 lines of interpretation for every line from Gorky. And when at long last the famous articles were finally published they had to be "chaperoned" by I. Vainberg's introductory article. I am not speaking of that critic's very valuable and informative notes and comments but specifically of the accompanying article that was almost half the length of Gorky's original work. I have no objection to the article itself which was precise, objective and decent in tone. Its very necessity, however, shows that we continue to fear Gorky's articles. Although there is no way out now: they at long last have been published.[1]

We may debate how successful this publication is. Vainberg did not take the newspaper articles but the book which Gorky made of them in 1918. The latter, however, did not include everything and its contents did not follow the original newspaper order of publication. For the book version, Gorky arranged the material by themes which were quite controversial: revolution, the people and culture; Russia, Europe and Asia ... This was not the main point, however, Gorky also mixed together articles written in the spring and autumn of 1917, thereby showing that *for him* the February revolution had in no way come to an end in October. So Vainberg could well cite the final will of the author as justification of his approach. Yet Gorky himself intended to produce a new edition of the book, adding to it other articles he had written then. In part he already did so in the Berlin edition of 1918 where certain of his *Untimely Thoughts* were linked to articles from other series of publications. He never produced this new edition in the 1920s and we shall not speculate as to the reasons, leaving that to his biographers. It is much more important for us as readers to follow the structure of these reflections and see how well they function *today.*

I do not think that Gorky's composition is now didactically effective. Such lessons quickly date but the experience remains. So it is not so much the conclusions that Gorky drew in 1918 or even the historical standing of this literary work that interests us striking though it may be. What we need is to examine how Gorky's thoughts evolved by offering a chronologically-ordered collection of his articles with the necessary commentary.

We may expect this to be done in the *Complete Works* which are now being published. Still, the literary work that Vainberg has reproduced here from the slim 1918 volume is an event of great importance.

* * *

The book reads as though it had been written today.

"Who is to blame for this devilish deceit and for creating this bloody chaos?" asked Gorky. "We shall not seek to blame others. Let us admit the bitter truth: we are all to blame for this crime, each and everyone of us..." I think this is an answer to the writer Vladimir Soloukhin. Recently he asked at what moment arrests and executions should be considered illegal and why he should share responsibility with those who were to blame for it all.

"Our belief is very easily given. The *narodniki* (19th-century Russian populists) described our peasant in growing terms and we eagerly believed that he was a wonderful creature, far above the European peasant ... Our peasants were universal beings! ... This Russian belief arises not from knowledge and love but just because it is comforting and less disturbing to think so. It is the faith of passive contemplation, fruitless and powerless ... Now that our people have freely disclosed to the world all the riches of their mentality, of attitudes taught by centuries of savage ignorance ... we begin to cry:

"'We do not believe in the people!'

"It would be appropriate to ask such faithless ones:

"'But why ever did you believe in them in the first place?'"

It takes some effort to realise that this was not written in reply to a round-table discussion devoted to the impoverishment (or, on the contrary, unending flow) of works by the "village prose" writers, extolling the virtues of simple Russian country folk.

"In Russia there are many who feel the pangs of conscience, even among professional thieves and murderers. They steal or kill their neighbour and then suffer remorse. A great many good and kind Russians find comfort in this remorse. They take such a feeble display of conscience as a sign of spiritual health when it is more probably a sign of an unhealthy lack of willpower"—at this point many of my contemporaries will interrupt and prevent Gorky from finishing what he has to say. How dare he criticise conscience, they object, and our heritage and our capacity for repentance ...

"These people evidently do not know that we have the best ballet in the world and the worst organised publishing business ... Siberia's newspapers, in a region abundant in forests, are actually printed on paper brought from Finland ... we transport cotton from Turkestan [Central Asia] to Moscow so that, after processing it, we may take it back from Moscow to Turkestan ..."

Or take the following quotation:

"They have lit a bonfire and it is burning poorly. It stinks of filthy, drunken and cruel Russia. Now this unhappy Russia is dragged and pushed to Golgotha to be crucified to save the world.... But the West is severe and mistrustful, and quite unsentimental ... It has a very simple way of assessing the individual: do you know how to work, or don't you? If the answer is 'no' then you are superfluous in the workshop of the world. And that's that. Since Russians do not like to work and do not know how to work, and since the Western world knows this very well, we shall have a very hard time of it, harder than we expect ..."

This comment directly supports the views of Vladimir Tsvetov (a long-serving Soviet TV correspondent in Japan) as to why the Japanese refused to set up joint enterprises in the Soviet Union.

The next remarks are just as relevant to our present-day cooperatives.

There was in 1918 a ban on publishing job offers and applications in the press. "Formerly you could pick up a newspaper and choose among offers of work for your particular skill. Now at the door of every trade union you are met by despicable smiles and offensive jokes, and there is no work to be had ..." "'offensive jokes' and rudeness in general have already become part of the new bureaucracy's way of operating ..." "It was bad enough in the past, if we're to be frank about it, and if the same happens now then it was hardly worth all that effort."

And one more passage about thuggery:

"In this verbal punch-up, which for decency's sake we term 'polemics', the contestants have no time for the truth. Instead they pick up each other's verbal slips ... not so much to prove the truth of their own beliefs as to give public display of their own agility ..." "If we compare the psychology of the lynch-mobs with the tactics used in newspaper 'polemics' we find that on the street and in the papers they are all blind and frantic people ... It is the mentality of those who cannot forget that 56 years earlier [1861 Emancipation of the Serfs,—Ed.] they were slaves ..."

Gorky also predicted how the people would react to such a form of glasnost:

"Seeing what aims are pursued through 'freedom of speech', these millions may easily develop a pernicious contempt for it. This will be a fateful mistake and take many years to correct."

Finally one comment on that "experiment" in world history:

"Russia is being used as experimental material and the Russian people are the horse which bacteriologists vaccinate with typhus so that it produces antibodies in its bloodstream ..."

* * *

There is something grotesque in all these perceptions. I'm afraid they are too accurate and have the effect of a conjuring trick that dumbfounds us, rather than providing relief. The reader may even find Gorky's *Untimely Thoughts* too "contemporary" and rejoice in this unexpected support in our topical disputes. In so doing, he or she will overlook the staggering profundity of Gorky's writings.

For they contain something infinitely more important and terrible than contemporary relevance, disclosed after 70 years. They describe a drama that refers directly to our own drama. Today it is more important for us to understand this than to pull the book to pieces, quoting selectively to find ammunition for our current polemics.

Take one episode from October 1917. The Bolsheviks issued the rallying cry, Be prepared. Gorky refused to fall in line. He considered that the working class should not take part in "comrade Trotsky's febrile dance on the ruins of the Russian empire": the mistakes and crimes of such leaders would be paid for with thousands of lives and rivers of blood.

A reply came from the Bolshevik camp, but not at all in "comrade Trotsky's dancing style". I shall give a condensed version so that you may feel the style and cold, calm tone of that response. However, you have only to look at Volume 3 of Stalin's *Collected Works* to see that this was indeed the tone adopted, and that it determined the style:

"The bourgeoisie has unveiled its cannons. We don't mind. *History will not forget the fact.* We shall reserve *special treatment* for the bourgeoisie and its echoing minions. As far as the hysterical journalists of *Novaya zhizn* are concerned, it is difficult to understand what they actually want from us. If they want to know on which day the uprising will occur so as to run away in good time then we can only praise them for this intention. We are above all in favour of clarity in such matters. If they want to know on which day the uprising will occur so as to calm their 'iron' nerves then we must assure them that this will not help. As soon as we Bolsheviks let them know this, on the side, they will throw a hysterical fit. If, on the other hand, they simply want to distance themselves from us then, again, we can only praise them for this: such a step will undoubtedly *be noted by the right people* if the uprising is a failure ..."

The icy tone of this statement must have hurt Gorky far more than any of its arguments. Did he know that the author of this editorial comment was none other than Stalin? Did he have any idea in 1917 what Stalin was like or even who he was? Even if he had not already distinguished Stalin he must have recognised the tone of that voice carrying across the sounds of that "febrile dance". Gorky had a writer's ear, after all. Moreover, some of it was addressed to him personally:

"The Russian Revolution has overthrown many authorities. Its strength was expressed, among other things, in its refusal to bow down to 'great names' and it either took them into its service or cast them into limbo if they did not want to learn from the Revolution. Plekhanov, Kropotkin, Breshkovskaya and Zasulich ... We fear that Gorky was envious of their reputations. We fear that Gorky was 'fatally' drawn to them, to the past ... Well, he may act as he pleases. ... The revolution does not pity or bury its corpses ..."

Then Gorky did not give way: "Be more humane in these days of universal descent into bestiality!" Yet the path would lead from these words to others he uttered in the 1930s: "If an enemy will not surrender, he is destroyed!" It would lead to slave labour on the White Sea Canal, to the concentration camp of Solovki, and the "reforging" of the backward masses into the "New Man". Gorky would become enraptured by the iron will of Joseph Stalin. How did this metamorphosis occur? or did Gorky really change? It is vitally important today to answer these questions.

Stylistic research offers some clues.

In 1917-1918 the left-radical press carried on a polemic against Gorky. He was criticised not only in *Pravda* but in other papers of similar view; not only in the Party press but also the government papers like *Izvestiya* and in general by the more or less free journalists and ordinary officials (not just those in Zinoviev's immediate entourage). It is not the ideas that astonish us in this attack (they were more or less widely accepted) so much as the dense and impenetrable figurative and mythological style in which they were cloaked. The proletariat "having cast off the chains of centuries of slavery will begin, with inexperienced but powerful arms, to build a new life". Meanwhile Gorky instead of "blending with them" strikes "the pose of an indifferent observer" and points out the scars and gaping wounds on the body of the liberated giant. It is impossible to cut through this imagery. Gorky complained that the distinguished and elderly actress Ermolova had been robbed and in reply was told that "the young warrior as he creates a new life takes away another's well-being with his muscled arms". When he spoke of the pillage of the Gatchina palace they talked of "smashing a millennial system", of "snivelling philistines" and even of the "stormy petrel" which had become a "loon".

This allegorical mist was so thick that it can hardly be attributed to purely stylistic origins. What style can we talk of, indeed: it is on the level of the crude popular broadside ballads and woodcut illustrations. Stalin's seminary training had given him rather better taste than the poets Kornilov and Demyan Bedny with their talk of "warriors" and "giants". Stalin's associations were biblical but, again, also shrouded in an ambiguous mist. It is impossible to see individual people through his clouds of metaphor. There are classes, detachments, armies and masses. Silhouettes and allegories. Enemies who naturally would not surrender, and fighters who destroyed them. It is difficult to pin down facts of a human scale in this mythological realm but Gorky tried. In *Untimely Thoughts,* he quoted from letters, described incidents and referred to eyewitness testimony. Here, however, one has the strange feeling that Gorky was also in essence not writing about facts but about something different that had already been separated and distilled from those facts. These letters and dialogues with eyewitnesses seem to continue Gorky's old, perpetual and unmistakably personal " philosophical debate" . "Aphorisms and maxims" succeed one another and all the factual accounts have already been passed through the prism of the indestructible Russian euphoria which originates not in fact but in some elevated vision. "I tell you, o friend of men, that what is happening in the villages is nonsense because the soldiers' wives are being given land ... and they are howling. When their husbands return from the war there will be a fight on this account, take my word for it ..." Involuntarily Gorky was distracted by the language and outlook of his correspondents. It is difficult for us to pin down any facts since they seem to hover and flutter in the air without substance and support. All talk of killing, deception and robbery is somehow abstract. "It is social idealism that moves the world," wrote Gorky. He considered that "intellectual maximalism is very good for the lax Russian soul". Yet the Bolshevik "people's commissars" surely thought exactly the same? They also were not without their "pure idealism" and believed that their experiment would liberate in man that *ideal* being who was thought to lie concealed beneath all the filth and baseness. How then could Gorky refute their experiments? How then could the anonymous readers in *Pravda* fail to accuse him of changing from a "stormy petrel" to a "loon" if in both incarnations he taught them about both the Falcon and the Serpent and other allegorical figures that surrounded the man? (Or, rather, we should say the Man with the capital M.)

It is through this rhetorical style that we discern the sailors killed early in 1918 and the resolution of revenge that followed. In March certain members of the shore brigade of the Russian Federation's Red Fleet were killed. "For each of our murdered comrades we shall take the lives of hundreds and thousands of the rich ..." Gorky was horrified by the subsequent orgy of hostage-taking. Yet how could this process be halted and investigated when there were neither investigations nor court-cases but only open-air meetings. There on the sport were those who had actually been murdered and their actual murderers and the elevated image of "our best comrades who died at the treacherous hands of the tyrants". In place of a sentence there went up the howl "For each of our heads, a hundred of yours! "

Gorky reasoned with the sailors in a style that combined abstract solemnity with a definite feeling of total helplessness: "Gentlemen sailors, you must come to your senses. You must try to be human beings. It is hard but it is essential."

The concealed sneer that we may detect today in Gorky's address to the "Gentlemen sailors" (an oxymoron in fact) was hardly intended. Or if it was, then it was not typical. He did not mock, he appealed. And his appeals were stubborn and hopeless:

"Let me say to you as mothers that hatred and malice are bad midwives." Thus he addressed the women on whom life now "depended" and who "are cursing the Bolsheviks, peasants and workers".

"Citizens, culture is in danger" ... "We must work, respected citizens, we must work—that is our only hope of salvation, there is none other!" ... "Be more humane in these days of a universal descent into bestiality ..."

Somehow he did not have much faith in his own appeals. "I know that there is not a soul who will accept these words ..." It was as if he was talking to children who have got out of hand and can no longer be restrained by a good whipping. But the whip itself is bad, a form of violence. So there he stood, and pronounced his words without belief. This hopelessness reached into some abyss rocking beneath the feet and into which it was impossible to shout. For there were no individuals there but only those same warriors and giants, cohorts, masses, classes, detachments and types. Gentlemen sailors, citizens, proletarians and snivelling philistines.

This was the drama of a great writer whose eyes were made for a particular vision: all the time his gaze slid from the individual to the outline of the Individual. He cursed, suffered and cried aloud his impotence. Nevertheless, he could not make himself heard.

This drama derives from the very roots of Russian reality.

The common people are terrifying, in Gorky's view, and the intelligentsia is powerless. The Russian people were an enormous flabby body while the Russian intelligentsia was a vast head unhealthily swollen with an abundance of alien thoughts. The two were joined not by a strong spine but by a barely discernible and fine thread of nerve. Nowhere did Gorky give such acute expression to such feelings as in his *Untimely Thoughts.* Our reader who can now read those articles will see that I have not distorted or exaggerated at all. The situation was one of mortal danger. For Gorky the people were an Asiatic element, a cruel and cunning hunted beast, an eternally rebellious slave who left his submissiveness and stupefaction not for freedom but for an anarchistic outburst, loutishness, and unreasoning craziness and revelry. According to the fatalistic logic of the East, the Russian was drawn, in Gorky's view, to an *equality of nonentities.* The Russian bungler sought those to blame elsewhere, anywhere else apart from in the abyss of his own stupidity.

These issues are now highly topical in our society and one can imagine the reaction Gorky's ideas will provoke in those today inclined to regard "the people" as the final guarantee of salvation. There is another traditional Russian way of thinking about the common people which derives from Dostoyevsky. Here the people must not be judged by the vile deeds they commit but by the spiritual purity they retain in all such vileness. One can marshal facts to support either of these views. Such an argument will be quite meaningless, to my mind, because it will be totally "mythological" in style. In essence, the subject is quite different. We should not be asking what conception of the "people" we shall imprint on our "banner" but how we must live, act and resolve the specific problems we face and in our real situation (with this head swollen with alien ideas and the universal loutishness of good people).

That was how Gorky looked at the problem as well. There is some sense in talking of a line of conduct, of the writer's destiny. Destiny dictated the line Gorky followed and he had grounds for regarding with horror all he saw around him. This horror he had carried from his childhood and boyhood from the "leaden vileness" of the disintegrating peasant way of life and the psychology of the city outskirts through which he had painfully made his way towards culture and learning.

He himself took almost a schoolboy or, rather better, a student's view of the enlightenment offered by this culture. Although the experiences Gorky ironically described as My *Universities* were extremely close to everyday life he nevertheless did see them explicitly as universities and derived from them a firm faith for the rest of his life: enlightenment and culture will save us. By this he meant European culture, experimental science, free art, modern equipment and so on ... Spiritual values were created by Reason. Suffering should be hated and instead one should apply one's intelligence . . .

Gorky derived this rational division of the spirit from the "Asiatic ignorance" which he relied on the direct action of "European enlightenment" to disperse. It made his truth optically acute but difficult to grasp. It is like a holographic image: the volume is visible, the contours precise but one "cannot touch" it: it is immaterial. Everything appears as in a magnifying glass—purity and romanticism, benighted ignorance and impenetrable gloom. Of course, Gorky would never have descended to the fairy-tale "warriors" and broadsheet "giants" if only because of his instinctive sense of form. In the very depths of his spirit, nevertheless, reality was seduced by form at its most diffuse: instead of the individual there towers the " Individual", optically enormous and of giddying size. How could the drunken, cunning Russian peasant, that hunted beast, attain such grandeur? By what suffering path could poor the Russian reach that goal if *suffering* was hated and forbidden? Alas, suffering was not the way, the people must grow up. The task was of an educational, almost quantitative, nature. Teachers and mentors were needed. Guidelines were needed. The "chains of culture" were needed, but they were frail and the "beast" would break loose. "Culturevaluable" people (as Gorky put it) were needed, the mind of the nation, the teachers of life but, as he wrote, they were being starved and deprived of food rations. The artists must break into the chaos of the street with the force of their gifts and pacify the crazed citizen. They would moderate his unruly conduct and ennoble his rampant instincts.

Artists appear particularly attractive and touching in this role. After 1910, not to mention the 1920s, Gorky could already have seen that whatever happened when artists broke into the chaos of the streets, they did so with no aims of pacification but rather revealed in such uproar, inflaming and guiding it to the stage of "worldwide conflagration". The scientists and scholars, Gorky's culture-valuable people, proved more honest when faced not so much by the chaos of life torn from its traditional moorings as by the instinctive hostility of the rioting mass towards intellect. Ideas were turned inside out and upside down; the intellectuals found themselves disoriented or powerless. They had no power to pacify chaos with Reason. Gorky then felt that a Will was needed.

Yet where might such a *will* be found in this diffuse realm? Gorky had a social guarantee of salvation in the "working class". Again this was a faith derived from his boyhood experience of artisan's workshops: metal was harder than earth. The manual worker was an aristocrat of democracy and a force for culture in a peasant country. Force ... Again in this mythological element the outline that appears to guarantee salvation is illuminated. Why do I say mythological, though: was the working class really not a reality in the particular *balance of forces* which Gorky was looking at and trying to understand?

It certainly was, but Gorky was crucially trying to glimpse something more than that in this balance of forces: he sought the resolution of a spiritual enigma. For him the "working class" was just such a mythological element that brought salvation and was logically comprehensible. And universal, moreover. In practice, everything did not follow the course his hero Pavel Vlasov had taken in *Mother.* This was not just because the "best workers" had been killed in the "accursed war" that preceded 1917. Nor was it simply because the proletariat when it began to act in 1917-1918 proved to be "not magnanimous or just" at all. Gorky saw all this. However, there was yet another circumstance which he did not see but, it seems, could sense. I shall try to convey it with a highly topical example.

When an Inter(national) Front was set up in one of the Baltic republics to counter the activities of the People's Front there it became clear that most of its members were skilled workers as opposed to the artistic and media people involved in the People's Front. I emphasise their qualifications because there was no great "disparity in levels" between the two: the modern highly-skilled worker is no less cultured than the middle-ranking journalist who makes up the main bulk of the People's Front membership. Nevertheless, as it turned out, the workers had lagged behind in setting up their Interfront. When asked why, one of them answered:

"I don't have a telephone on my lathe: if I did I could also ring up my supporters while at work ..."

This refers to our own days when a worker is likely to have a computerised control panel on his lathe, so what can one suppose about the "unforgettable year of 1919"?

It is not a question of the tasks people perform or of their social background. But when they have to play a different role individuals must be free to do so, i.e. the manual worker must leave his lathe because *liberty* must have free hands.

Gorky had no alternative. The working class produced from its own environment a special force in order to prevent the people from collapsing into chaos. This particular force, incidentally, could gather into itself members of the intelligentsia and the peasantry. Gorky's attitude to the various embodiments of this force varied; yet he had no doubts that such a force was essential. As things turned out, he had his differences with the "party", arguing with Lenin and being openly hostile towards Zinoviev. Yet the Cheka men of State Security, however, seemed to have only appeared to him in a heroic light. In the end, the *"iron will"* of Stalin inevitably found its way to his heart.

We may seek reasons for the inevitable and natural character of this outcome in Gorky's mistakes. A great man, he was trying to resolve a task more than any single human might bear. For us, nevertheless, this is not the primary issue. We must ask why he tried to resolve a task that was beyond his strength. Why such stubbornness of the spirit and resistance?

It was dangerous to argue with such a regime: he who did not surrender was indeed destroyed.

It was fatally dangerous to stand in the path of the advancing masses. Whipped up by these ideas, they did not pay attention to subtleties and swept aside any who stood in their way.

When the regime and the masses worked in unison it was not simply fatal to resist, it was almost senseless. Neither the cynics nor the looters could be distinguished when people were fanatically inspired by a truly great and pure idea and nothing could be set against it.

Furthermore, all his life the writer had himself served this idea. Gorky's psychological position was especially complex. It might seem that his influential reputation, authority and popular fame would give him the strongest of trump cards. In fact, they all had another and negative aspect: he was expected to behave in quite a different way. Millions had become accustomed to thinking of Gorky as the "grave-digger on the old world" and saw any attempt by him to save the next doomed member of the intelligentsia as an act in favour of that "old world"—it was a betrayal, it was treason. It is possible to stand up against hatred but how easy is it to resist a deceiving love? Gorky did not even begin his resistance from

a neutral position but from a negative one in which his authority actually complicated his resistance.

Yet resist he did.

His efforts in 1917-1918 leave the impression of a titanic struggle. The
mistakes were an inseparable part of this struggle. It was impressive not in spite
of but because of these mistakes which were both false and real, and because of
his romantic illusions. For without the latter the great drama of Gorky's life would
not have taken place. Nothing can be corrected here, it must all just be endured.

This lesson is incomparably more important for us today than how ap-
posite Gorky's insights are to our concerns 70 years later. As the reader has noted,
I delight in pointing out their relevance. The reader also can see that I do not
gloat over Gorky's illusions. The main lesson of his position is not to be found by
exposing these illusions. Today it is easy for us to account for them, and we note
his weakness more with our minds than our hearts.

With our hearts, we sense the grandeur of this man for whom the dignity
of the individual was an *absolute* value. This was more important than a position
which may be adjusted, or a topicality that will pass. It is more important than
"principles" in which it is easy to become psychologically snared: we have seen
plenty of people in our history who stubbornly "cannot compromise their principles". We can use anything for our topical needs and adjust our positions most
splendidly. It is greatness of spirit that we lack today. If we possess that attribute
then all the rest may be discussed; different versions and paths of action are then
possible. The source of resistance is what is important. It must be above selfish-
ness and particular interests—they are "something else".

In Gorky's articles there is much reference to this "something else".
There are many relevant and fruitful ideas there. For example, on January 5, 1918
Gorky protested against the arrest of Irakli Tsereteli, the Menshevik and member
of the Constituent Assembly. In passing he commented that Civil War, or the
self-destruction of democracy, was a consequence of the substitution of "the theoretical triumph of anarcho-syndicalist ideas" in place of the "practical interests of
the working class". It is the insight that theory is flouting reality which is intrigu-
ing in this remark. The experiment was running counter to experience. It was not
that the ideas were anarcho-syndicalist and the interests, those of the working
class: any ideas were capable of infringing the interests of any individual, be he
worker, peasant or intellectual. Ideas might "in theory be right", what was important was people's practical readiness to understand them correctly. For this a
school was needed, the long school of democracy and economic management...
This idea was not developed in Gorky's writings and only accompanied his main
struggle for the Individual and Reason, the Proletariat and the Intelligentsia. If
Gorky had only moved a little further from the romantic symbolism which had
helped him stand up straight even in boyhood; if he had approached instead a

sense of the specific social realities and empirical facts of the life led by his drowsy Russian (whose riotous behaviour so tormented him); then Gorky would have already gone through an experience still close but already different to that he knew. For this, however, a different writer was needed.

* * *

As you may guess, I am referring to Vladimir Korolenko (1853-1921) whose six astonishing letters to Lunacharsky in 1920 have at last reached our public.[2] He wrote these letters just before his death and these last works by a great Russian writer are comparable in their importance, their power to influence and their depth of understanding to the resurrected articles of Gorky. For our *present* literature their publication is also an event of great and far-reaching significance.

It was Korolenko who developed the thought that ideas had then "theoretically triumphed" over the "practical" possibilities of contemporary reality. "The ideas are one and the same," he commented, "a social upheaval and a rapid march to socialism. Yet an interesting law comes into play here, for the less prepared a society is, the more decisive these visionaries are. American socialists are not in such a hurry. They consider that capitalism has still not done all it can, i.e. it has not raised the economy to the necessary level. The Rumanians, by contrast, in a country which is still far from reaching that stage, are ready to stage such a putsch without dawdling. While in their impoverished country the Russians have already begun. The experiment is underway. The English socialists regard it without enthusiasm. The Turkish socialists, on the other hand, send Russia 'greetings from the fanatical East': 'in the squares before the mosques ... wandering dervishes call on their squatting listeners to wage a holy war against the Europeans and, at the same time, send greetings to the Russian Soviet republic... One can hardly say that is a case of progress as Marx and Engels envisaged it,' commented Korolenko with bitter irony. 'Probably it is quite the opposite: Asia responds to that in us to which it feels akin, to our Asiatic inclinations ...'"

There is an obvious echo of Gorky here. The actual fabric of Korolenko's thought, however, was different and had another foundation. His journalistic style was an inimitable combination of scholarly and well-founded ideas delicately intertwined with emotional reactions to these same ideas. He himself took these ideas seriously and not in the slightest degree romantically. For him they were practical matters and he had devoted his life to their promotion: he thought and lived in these same categories and treated them precisely as scholarly concepts not symbols and anti-symbols. When Gorky could see nothing more than the "simplified translations of anarcho-communist slogans into the language of our native aspens" (symbol on symbol), Korolenko sought for the real meaning. He did not compare certain words with others, nor symbols with other symbols—he compared real conditions and real things. For him the freedoms of "assembly, conscience, speech and the press" meant real elements in everyday life and not the imagined shores of the distant future. It was of course pure savagery to his ears when he heard that these were all "bourgeois superstitions": "Only we who have never fully known these liberties and have not learnt to use them together with the people declare them to be 'bourgeois superstitions' that merely hold back the cause of justice."

"It is a vast mistake on your part," he wrote to Lunacharsky, "to talk in this way. It constantly recalls the Slavophil myth of our 'god-bearing' people. It is even more reminiscent of Ivanushka in the Russian fairy tale: thanks to the magic pike he was able to surpass all learning and science without having any learning himself, and do everything without stirring a finger. The very ease with which you have managed to draw our popular masses after you does not show how ready we are for socialism but, on the contrary, how immature our people are..." "The Russian nation has still not learnt how to cast votes, or how to give voice to the prevalent public opinion. It has begun to build social justice by individual acts of robbery (that's your slogan: 'steal back the stolen') and inaugurated the kingdom of justice by allowing mass shootings without trial that have been going on for several years now. Such a nation is still far from ready to lead the best aspirations of mankind. It should be learning things itself and not teaching others..." "You have not created anything but have destroyed a great deal. To put it another way, by rapidly introducing communism you have discouraged for a very long time even the desire for simple socialism when the latter is the most urgent need of the modern world..."

Today we are struck by the sobriety of Korolenko's vision. He could perceive this reality in 1920, a year obscured by the smoke and fire of the Civil War, oppressed by destruction and blinded by hatred.

We are struck by the direct way he apparently speaks to Anatoli Lunacharsky but through him, in fact, is addressing the Bolsheviks, real and tangible listeners whom he wanted and hoped to convince. Gorky shared no such hope. His ironical addresses (We must work, respected citizens! Come to your senses, gentlemen sailors) owed much more to a figurative sermon than to any practical programme. Korolenko, on the other hand, really wanted his cry to be heeded.

We are struck by Korolenko's proximity to the facts and his confidence in his own capacity to see and hear. He was ready to rely on the kind of empirical reality from which Gorky's thoughts recoiled in grief-stricken disorder. Korolenko's letters are not just a great piece of writing, they also give a true picture of life in Poltava in 1920: they are accurate, well-documented—and apocalyptic. This is not only the case with those horrifying events like execution without trial but in daily life as well. Potatoes had been planted but were stolen straight from the garden before they were ripe. So their owner had to dig them up when they were still unripe; but unripe potatoes do not keep, so they rotted and he was left with no reserves. "I've seen a group of poor women who in the morning stood and cried over their vegetable beds which had been grubbed up in the night. They had worked, and planted, banked up the plants and hoed round them. Then others had come along and ripped up the plants, trampled much else and dug up the potatoes which needed two more months before they were ripe. And this was all in the space of an hour." There you have it: some had worked and others had enjoyed the fruits of their labour. Moreover, these "others" were actually from one and the same background, from the same social origin. This was the horror of it. "A large part of the harvest grown by our nation 'under communism' has perished directly due to our present morality." Korolenko did not deceive himself with words. He looked at what was happening and could not be distracted from that terrible spectacle.

God moves, as the Bible says, in a mysterious way. Thirty years earlier in Nizhny Novgorod the 20-year-old Alexei Peshkov (later to call himself Maxim "the Bitter" or Gorky) brought his first verse to Korolenko for "advice and instruction". Thanks to the then exiled writer, Gorky's very first stories were sent to *Russkoe bogatsvo,* a Petersburg journal he could not himself have aspired to. Korolenko helped him to get printed in the major literary periodicals.

Then they became equals, both in literature and in public life. Korolenko was a recognised champion of the oppressed and unjustly accused: he successfully defended the Udmurts accused of human sacrifice in the Multan village affair, saved the Chechen Yusupov from execution and never hesitated to protest against pogroms and other acts of oppression.

Sometimes they fought side by side, for instance in the Beilis case when a Jew was accused of ritual murder of Christian children. In 1917 and 1920 they were also in essence fighting shoulder to shoulder. Thereafter their paths divided. Korolenko would soon die of a chill in the futility of Poltava's provincial devastation. After living in Sorrento Gorky would return in the late 1920s to his "native aspens", to visit the Solovki concentration camp and the White Sea Canal and closer to the Kremlin.

Yet even Korolenko's case was not entirely futile and hopeless. His position was incomparably weaker than Gorky's in 1918. The latter had a newspaper and a tribune from which he could daily influence a great many people. Korolenko could only write letters, moreover private letters, that had not the slightest chance of being published in Russia.

But what about publication in Europe? Korolenko's position was a curious mixture of glasnost and lack of glasnost. Lunarcharsky made no reply to any of these letters but, it appears, Korolenko did not expect him to. Moreover, it seems likely that Lunacharsky deliberately "provoked" their appearance so that this outstanding writer would speak his mind. And it had been Lenin who prompted Lunarcharsky to start this one-sided correspondence. It is hard to say whether only Lunarcharsky read the letters or whether he passed them directly on to Lenin. However, we know that the latter read them later in 1922 when they were published in book form in Paris.

We cannot say whether Korolenko intended his letters more for publication abroad *(tamizdat)* or, to use contemporary dissident jargon, in *samizdat.* Before they appeared in Paris they had already circulated in Russia in manuscript form. In either case, he was not writing in a vacuum, without any hope of being read.

But what if even these possibilities were denied the individual? Suppose that a Russian or Soviet newspaper, even after strict censorship, would not publish such comments or that a foreign publisher, even one very far away, would not accept these articles for publication. In those negative circumstances, could an individual still find the resolution to say all that he or she believed?

He could.

In the mid-1930s Ivan Pavlov, the world-renowned physiologist, who was then 85, wrote to the Soviet government protesting against the massive wave of dismissals and arrests. This was immediately after the fateful assassination of Kirov in December 1934. The elderly Academician possessed nothing but his experimental dogs in Koltushi—and even for them he had to go cap in hand asking for their feed. He had no newspaper like Gorky in 1918, no typography in the West, and no literary style that would ensure his text (like Korolenko's) at least private circulation. The old man wrote all the same, although it was like talking to a brick wall:

"It is my profound conviction that what is called 'wrecking' is for the most part, if not exclusively, a consequence of people's decline in interest and energy and not a conscious activity directed against an undesirable regime..."

"...What you are doing is, of course, only an experiment, however vast in its boldness ... and ... like any experiment, the final result is as yet unknown. Secondly, it is a terribly costly experiment (and this is its essence) that is destroying any cultural calm and all the cultural beauty of life..."

"...I see a similarity between our life and the life of the ancient Oriental despotisms. But we call our system republican. What can one make of that? One may say, perhaps, that all this is temporary. Yet we must remember that man evolved from a beast and that it is easy to relapse but difficult to raise one's self again..."

"This is a fact that is quite evident and universal, both in large and in small matters ..."

These letters did not possess the literary style that would have assured their wider private circulation. They had only one reader in mind, Vyacheslav

Molotov, the head of the Soviet government to whom they were addressed. On being received they were first placed in a file and then transferred to an ultra-secret restricted-access library where they "cannot be found" to this day. Unlike Molotov, Pavlov preserved the replies of the prime minister in his scholarly personal archive.

The meaning of Molotov's replies is clear: this is none of your business, much respected Academician. We as political leaders do not interfere in your scientific affairs.

This was, in the first place, untrue. Politicians interfered in biology to such an extent in 1948 in supporting Lysenko that today we must still buy grain from the West. Secondly, it is an extraordinary conviction that mass political repression was the business of politicians and did not concern anyone else. Pavlov thought otherwise. He believed that the terror and "unrestrained despotism of the authorities" affected everyone, himself included. He considered that this lawlessness was transforming "our already sufficiently Asiatic character into something shamefully servile", and protested. No scientific interests required him to do so (in this Motolov was right). It was a question of dignity, plain and simple. Yet Pavlov was thereby risking his life. And it is an illusion to say that they would not have dared to touch him. The world-wide fame of the biologist Nikolai Vavilov did not prevent them letting him die in 1943 in Saratov prison hospital .

Some have passed on the opinion of one of the doctors attending him that Pavlov was indeed murdered. This has also been said of the others I have mentioned here. Soloukhin says it of Korolenko: he had hardly fallen ill when doctors arrived from Moscow who helped dispatch him to the next world And since we were children we have heard that Gorky was similarly helped to the grave. At first the poisoners were "Zinovievite-Bukharinist monsters" and then this accusation was dropped, but the monstrous act remained.

I somehow have no urge to delve into these detective-story proposals. If so many millions were then being put to death this was in the nature of things. What difference does it make, moreover, if they simply waited for these three elderly men to die of their own accord? !

They could not have changed the overall situation. A single individual is incapable of doing so. The issue I have raised is different: how does the individual behave in such circumstances? Nothing then remained but dignity and dignity is such an intangible and imperceptible inconsequence. Individual dignity is an issue that we must face today and, I fear, will continue to face in the future.

Some now claim that Pavlov was motivated to protest by his "religious convictions". This is untrue. He was an atheist-rationalist and said so quite clearly. It was in response to the atheistic terror against Christian believers in 1918 that he began to "cross himself in front of every church he passed". There was a method in his manner. It was when people were punished for wearing their tsarist awards and medals that he began to wear his; before the Revolution he had not bothered to parade in them. It was the same logic that led him to write directly to the Soviet government and never appeal to "international public opinion". The Soviet authorities could rest assured that Pavlov would never stab his country in the back at any international congress although he had such opportunities. No, when he was abroad he defended his country and preferred to tell the truth to her face, not behind her back.

We are not discussing positions here but something that does not depend on a position at all. As a person with a particular position, by the way, I find the socialist Korolenko more attractive than Pavlov with his search for human reflexes that corresponded to those he had discovered in dogs. Closest of all to my heart is Gorky, whom I have understood, loved and pitied ever since I first read him. If we are to speak of dignity, however, and the stature of the individual then this order of preference should be reversed. Perestroika has caused an upheaval in our journalistic values and taught us to see in literature not the beauty and perfection of a text but the trace and meaning of the individual's presence. In this sense, the partial publication of Pavlov's letters[3] in the newspaper *Sovetskaga kultura is* an event of immeasurable moral significance for our public discussions, our literature and our present self-awareness. We must be able to draw the lesson, though.

A famous anecdote tells how a Leningrad militiaman, recently drafted in from the village, shook his head at the sight of Pavlov demonstratively crossing himself in front of a church: what benighted ignorance!

We must try to not be like that militiaman today. This is particularly necessary when positions are shifting so profoundly. The Millennial Celebration of the Baptism of Russia in 1988 has led us to a passionate reconciliation with the Orthodox church but, as usual, everyone has joined in rather indiscriminately.

I shall conclude with a curious episode in which the paths of my three heroes cross for the last time.

In some memoir or other I have read that Gorky, on meeting Pavlov immediately after the Revolution, expressed his astonishment that the latter believed in God. It must have struck Gorky as strange from every point of view, both in personal terms and considering Pavlov's membership of the Academy of Sciences. The latter reason mattered even more to him than the former. (Incidentally, Gorky himself almost became an Academician. Before the Revolution his narrow failure to be elected caused Korolenko to reject his own title of honorary Academician in protest.) Gorky retained understanding reverence for the Academy throughout his life.

Gorky suggested to Pavlov that there was a much more real and worthy object of rapture than God: the outstanding individual. He could, moreover, see just such an individual standing before him. As proof of his words, Gorky reportedly took off his hat and bowed deeply before Pavlov. The latter flew into an un-describable rage. Gorky left him, aware that he had offended him in some way, but hardly able at that moment to understand exactly why.

Even if this story is apocryphal it is quite splendid.

It will do us no harm today to understand the difference between god and man; and we must distinguish between a position, which we may call all "fellow-thinkers" to support with "all their might", and the dignity and rights of the individual where we should not intervene even as individuals without permission (let alone "with all our might").

We should receive this lesson in dignity from our elders, who paid so dearly for their right to teach us.

NOTES

[1] M. Gorky, *Untimely Thoughk: Notes on Revolution and Culture:* first Soviet publication in *Literaturnoe obozrenie,* Nos. 9, 10 & 12, 1988; English trans., New York, 1968.

[2] V. Korolenko, Letters to A. V. Lunacharsky, *Novy mir,* No. 10, 1988. 1 say "the Soviet public" because readers abroad already had the Russian original in 1922.

[3] I. Pavlov, "I Protest Against Unrestrained Despotism", *Sovetskaya kultura,* January 14, 1989. The letters have been prepared for publication in fllll in the *Neva journal.*

ANTI-UTOPIA. THE 20TH CENTURY

Alexei Zverev[*]

The majority of Soviet readers, until very recently, only knew the famous anti-utopian works of Orwell and Huxley, and of their own compatriots Zamyatin and Platonov, by name. Few of them had been able to read *Animal Farm, 1984, Brave New World, We, Chevengur* and *The Foundation Pit.* Then in the space of only a year and a half they were all serialised and published in Russian journals. All had been originally published 50 and more years before when they might well have seemed no more than the fantasy of their authors' fevered imaginations. For their first readers they often appeared theoretical projections, and that was all. Today, however, we can compare these predictions with real experiences. Naturally they were not right about everything. Yet they were far too close to the truth for there to remain the slightest doubt that their authors' anxieties had been well founded.

For all readers today, but especially in the Soviet Union, they contain more of past history than of the future. So we do not perceive the "brave new world" of omnipotent technology as did Huxley's first readers in 1932. What for them was a speculative invention today strikes us almost as reality, or at least something that could happen in the very near future. What then seemed no more than artistic license now appears to be only a slightly distorted possibility. The sense of hyperbole has gone and instead we have the feeling that the writer had somehow jumped across the decades to our own time.

With whom was Zamyatin arguing when he wrote *We?* Which of the utopian visions was Huxley exposing when he created his *Brave New World?* Against which utopian writers did Platonov direct the emotional force of his *Chevengur?*

[*] **A. Zverev,** D.Sc. (Philol.). Author of the books: *Modernism in US Literature: The American Novel of the 1920s-1930s; The Melancholy Sunny World of Saroyan* and of a number of articles on modern literature abroad.

We may rack our brains to decide which famous utopian doctrines were the target of each work. It is very unlikely that we shall understand any of these books, however, if we adopt such an approach. They were not quarrelling with abstract conceptions but trying to understand a reality in which an attempt has been made to put utopian ideas into practice. Often the result appears quite fantastic but this is not just due to the logic of grotesque exaggeration which is an essential part of each anti-utopia. More important is the logic of life itself. This forces the speculative project to reveal itself fully. The anti-utopia is by its very nature an experiment in social diagnosis. All these imaginary islands, planets and historical epochs, and the parable form of narrative are merely the literary means that help to make the diagnosis as accurate as possible. Such precision is especially important because of the nature of the afflictions that the best anti-utopian works are trying to uncover and define. Almost always these sicknesses are among the most dangerous we face, although the symptoms can still hardly be detected when the anti-utopian expose is first written. Unfortunately, the dangers only become apparent decades later.

The lot of the authors of many such works is therefore a very hard one. Their contemporaries either ignored them or simply did not want to listen to their message. This is to some extent quite natural: prophets are without honour in their own country, and the epoch in which they are fated to live does not recognise them either. Time must pass, and often much time, before it is acknowledged how right they were.

* * *

The fate of Evgeni Zamyatin after he had written *We* fully confirmed this unwritten but seemingly inevitable law. Anti-utopian writers are first stoned and only later, usually posthumously, do they become revered as prophets. In Zamyatin's case this was almost literally his fate. In 1924, *We* was published abroad without the author's knowledge. Thereafter he was systematically and deliberately persecuted until in 1931 he was forced to leave Russia.

In the West the situation was different. However, the assessment, interpretation and perception of his novel were effectively the same. In the Soviet Union Zamyatin was humiliated while in the West he was adulated. If we are talking about how *We* was understood, however, these extreme reactions were not so very different. Everywhere he was seen as hostile to the prospects then opening before the new Russia. Whether this aroused indignation or rapture depended entirely on the politics of those discussing his book.

Subsequently, it is true, Western critics took a less crude view of Zamyatin. The appearance of Huxley's *Brave New World* in 1932 clarified the picture: Zamyatin's themes were too audible here to be ignored and the English writer, moreover, did not conceal that reading *We* had given him the original impetus and idea for his own work. Soon there would be a whole shelf-full of anti-utopias that took up the same conflicts and ideas. The most famous of these was B. F. Skinner's *Walden Two* (1947), an American psychologist's profoundly gloomy parable of the death of all that was natural and whole at the hands of a triumphant and aggressive technocracy.

Zamyatin was not just a classic but a pioneer in the fictional scourging of the technocrats and their rationalist obsession. He first described that hell which would reign on earth when nature's last hour had come.

Northrop Frye, the noted Canadian critic, has written that without Zamyatin there would have been no Huxley or Orwell. This is a great compliment coming from Frye; no other 20th-century Russian authors have earned the same praise from his lips. Yet why did he consider Zamyatin so important? Because he created a "utopian satire" of a "particular kind". It can only be the product of modern technological society with "its growing sense that the whole world is destined to the same social fate with no place to hide, and its increasing realisation that technology moves towards the control not merely of nature but of the operations of the mind."[1]

When Frye wrote this in 1965 such views of Zamyatin were still not widely accepted. Today they are a truism in the West. But does this say everything about the novel itself? Is that really its subject or, to be more accurate, is that all it is about?

When *We* was at long last published in Zamyatin's own country the first critical reaction was in some ways similar to Frye's interpretation. In his introduction to the novel published in journal form, Vladimir Lakshin spoke of the "author's techno-futuristic fantasy which started to become reality far sooner than he himself had anticipated."[2]

Zamyatin's futuristic predictions are today uncomfortably close to reality. Yet his prophetic vision was not restricted to an accurate forecast of the contemporary aggression of the technocratic way of thinking. This was not what distinguished *We* from all that had gone before.

Throughout the novel runs his persistent thought about what happens when all render obeisance to the ideal of an absolutely expedient and rational existence. He shows what happens to the individual, the state and the human community when liberty is rejected for the sake of this ideal and happiness is equated with servile subordination.

Such a thought was indeed new, at least for the anti-utopia. And it required, as Zamyatin fully appreciated, a quite unusual form of narrative to turn it into genuine literature. Intuition was quite alien to him. It might seem that the very subject matter, first and foremost, demanded intuition of the writer. Instead the novel is based on precise calculation and a kind of geometry that would thereafter become a distinctive feature of the genre.

In an article written in 1923 on the "New Russian Prose" Zamyatin asserted: "Life itself has today ceased to be unidimensional, It is no longer restricted within the former fixed boundaries but by the dynamic coordinates of Einstein and of revolution. In this new dimension the most usual of formulas and objects are displaced, fantastic and both familiar and strange at the same time. Hence that quite logical striving in today's literature towards the fantastic theme or to a fusion of reality and fantasy."[3] To support this he quoted many examples from Western literature and a few from Russian works: Ehrenburg's *Julio Jurenito,* Alexei Tolstoy's science fiction writings, and some of the first works of the Serapion Brotherhood (V. Kaverin, L. Lunts). And there was also, of course, his own *We.*

We should see no lack of modesty in Zamyatin's reference to his own novel. It was merely an acknowledgement of the new current in literature that had arisen under the influence of the revolution in society and in the sciences. Moreover it was not just that the narrative form had shifted towards a mixture of the fantastic and the real. Much more important was the direct connection Zamyatin made with a life that had changed beyond all recognition, even in everyday matters. The events in his anti-utopia took place in the distant future but its key ideas were bound up with what was happening in front of the author's eyes, here and now. It seemed to be his theorisation, a guess or attempt at prediction. In essence it was an intense examination of the "capricious and fantastic fairy-tale of history", to use Herzen's words,[4] unfolding against the powerful roar of the very recent revolution. Life had been turned upside down and had not yet regained settled, firm and durable form.

Once we have detected the vital presence of revolutionary Russia in Zamyatin's novel we must begin to examine it in a different light. In a thousand years people would raise up sinister technical wonders that would ruin them. Yet these proved far less interesting and important in *We* than the anxieties Zamyatin felt today when faced by that raging reality. If we retain a more or less visual picture of that reality such a proposition may seem far-fetched. The ruined, cold and swollen-bellied hunger of the country had no time for cosmic machines and superswift underground railways. However, we must remember that the dizziest aspirations were quite as typical of that time as ruin and poverty. Was it true to say, moreover, that Zamyatin was interested in the structure of the mechanised Single State only for its own sake? (A state that was "divinely set apart" by its Green Wall from the "irrational and ugly world of trees, birds and flowers".) Was his imagination also limited to that "indestructible eternal glass" of the cities of the future, or to the "vastly magnificent ballet of engines"[5] that would be considered the height of beauty there?

Zamyatin's City of the Sun is depicted with details that are too colourful and exotic for the time. It is hard to resist the temptation of today's reading of the book: it seems an astonishing prophecy of a society which has turned a primitive consumerism, crude pleasures and the triumph of social engineering into its fetishes. But this is only a part of his vision. The book also contains prophecy of another kind and quality. This should have prompted readers to understand *We* as a prognosis of the historical drama that had begun in the Soviet Union while Zamyatin was still living there.

Dogmatic criticism dealt Zamyatin its severest blows in autumn 1929, five years after the book was published abroad. The timing was no accident: it was the year of the Great Change which marked the assertion of Stalinism. The author was accused of slandering the revolution but the real reason for his persecution then was different: his novel had foreseen the possibility of Stalin's violence against the revolution. As soon as it became clear quite how accurate his forebodings were, the campaign intensified. The picture he created ceased to be the abstraction it might have earlier seemed and became recognisable. Zamyatin became unacceptable not because of the seditious parallels in his work with certain aspects of the new system of relations introduced by Stalinism: no, it was his ability to predict its very essence that caused alarm and anger.

Nothing in the book could suit-the enthusiastic supporters of that system, starting with the very title of the book. The author had unmasked his intentions, it was said, when he called the book *We*. He had in mind the common people who had made the revolution and presented them in a distorting mirror. In Zamyatin's work, however, "we" were not the masses but a social quality. Any type of individuality whatsoever was excluded in the Single State. The very possibility of becoming "I" and in some way separating from "we" was crushed. There remained only the faceless, enthusiastic mob which was easily moulded to the iron will of the Benefactor. The cherished idea of Stalinism was to transform the individual into a "bolt" in the vast machine of state which was controlled by the firm hand of its engineer or driver. Zamyatin showed this idea in practice. This alone would have sufficed for *We* to be acknowledged as a truly prophetic book.

The most important theme appears immediately with the first entry made by the narrator, in his very first paragraph. (Names have long ago been abolished as an expression of the criminal urge to be distinctive so Zamyatin's narrator is called D-503.) He quotes from the state Newspaper—evidently no others exist: "You will have to subordinate yet unknown beings inhabiting other planets, perhaps still living in a wild state of freedom, to the beneficial yoke of reason. If they do not understand that we are bringing them a mathematically infallible happiness then it is our duty to force them to be happy."

The writer of the newspaper article, of course, does not guess that he is almost repeating the Great Inquisitor's assertion that man could not become

happy until he had overcome freedom. For the subjects of the Single State Dostoyevsky is just so much derisible nonsense, like the rest of the culture man has
accumulated over thousands of years. It became unnecessary from that "blessed"
moment when the "perfect world" hidden behind the Green Wall was declared the
supreme achievement of creation.

Zamyatin himself saw how dreams of serene harmony were accompanied
by attacks on "unruled" freedom and "defective" morality. Such ideals would be
an ever more active force in all that went on around him. It is not so much that
the scenes described in We coincide with the actual course of events in Russia
after Lenin's death. But Zamyatin was the first to feel the threat of what would
later be called Stalinism. He understood the basic idea if he did not grasp its political origins.

There was to be a "single and powerful organism composed of millions
of cells ... a single Church". However, its sacred significance had been excluded
by the cares of the state or, to be still more accurate, by the interests of the Benefactor who knew the path that would lead all its cells to happiness. No one would
know this bliss as long the spectre of intellectual freedom remained. Therefore the
body of "unseen Wardens here in our ranks", proved essential: "they could in-
stantly establish the numbers of those who had become deluded and save them
from further false steps, and the Single State from them."[6] No one could rightly
consider themselves happy until they had a guarantee that they would not share
the fate of the three freedmen. As an experiment these three had been allowed not
to work for a month and on the tenth day, in a fit of depression, had committed
suicide.

Slave labour was to become a vocation and inner need. It would be a
norm of social life that the cells were quite indistinguishable; their nakedly functional existence was the guarantee of imperturbable social harmony and stability.
Imagination and the soul were inadmissible categories in the Single State because
they contradicted all its basic principles. D-503's lobotomy was justified for his
own good. "To say that 'I' had 'rights' of any kind in relation to the State was just
the same as saying that a gramme could equal a ton. Hence the ton was allocated
rights and the gramme, obligations. The path from insignificance to majesty was
natural: you would forget you were a gramme and instead feel yourself a millionth
part of a ton."[7] It is hard to believe, knowing the slogans and principles of Stalinism, that this was written in the early 1920s.

This was how the "early dream of paradise" was put into practice in
Zamyatin's novel, an Eden where "they no longer had any desires nor did they
know either pity or love."[8] Yet the Benefactor and his Wardens did not manage to
completely root out these atavistic feelings; neither could he cauterise their dissat-
isfaction and hostility to the happiness, in which like in iron collar they were being fettered. When Zamyatin was accused of hating socialism, this not only

equated socialism and the Stalinist system: it also ignored the novel's artistic nature as a grotesque narrative. It also deliberately overlooked a very important theme of conflict in the book, indicated by the subject of resistance. Even under conditions of mindless mass enthusiasm and a universal senselessness individuals did not cease to resist. Understandably this theme could not become central to *We* because Zamyatin's artistic purpose was different. Nevertheless this theme was present.

Zamyatin is now considered one of those writers who very early recognised the outlines of the totalitarian system soon to become a reality in several different countries. After reading a French translation of *We* in 1946 George Orwell commented that the book's most astonishing achievement was its "intuitive grasp of the irrational side of totalitarianism—human sacrifice, cruelty as an end in itself, the worship of a Leader who is credited with divine attributes."[9] Few others, in Orwell's view, had so perceptively understood the main danger presented by modern civilisation: that it demanded a constantly improving technology and valued man least of all.

If we are talking about the main conflicts in *We* this is a quite one-sided interpretation. However, Orwell seems to have been the only one capable of appreciating Zamyatin's idea that opposition would inevitably be born in the very depths of such a regime, although the latter did all it could to remove the very idea of freedom. For those who shared the experiences of Orwell in the 1930s time shifted the emphasis of Zamyatin's vision. Orwell fought in Spain and witnessed the internal repressions that fatally weakened the Republican Army. His generation was attracted to Zamyatin's book because it showed the means used for dealing with an opposition, however timid and inconsistent the latter might be. The novel's hero intended to start a revolution but was quickly broken by his visit to the Benefactor. He told the ruler all the names (or rather numbers) of those he knew to be "enemies of happiness" and this would be painfully reminiscent of what happened in the 1930s. However, in that atmosphere the theme of disagreement was perhaps still more important although it was rewarded with torture, forced repentance and the moral ruin of the disobedient.

Whatever importance Zamyatin attributed to this theme it could not be altogether absent. It was essential to the anti-utopia as a genre. Otherwise the result would not have been literature but a discussion of social organisation. Thomas More and Campanella continue to be included among utopian novelists although it is quite arbitrary, for the above reason, to describe their works as novels. The modern anti-utopia, beginning with Zamyatin, is quite another matter. As he himself said, *We* was an experiment in synthesising art and philosophy and for the work to have genuinely literary features there had to be a central conflict. The solution was very obvious. The hero must have doubts about the logical presuppositions of a system that strives, like the engineers of the Single

State, to make man entirely "machine-like". He must experience these doubts as the culminating episode in his life even when the final outcome proves tragic and seemingly unavoidable. Zamyatin thus describes the operation which ensured that his hero would now always be "certain that we shall triumph. Because reason must triumph."[10]

If the anti-utopia is a work of art such a conflict must arise. The artistic conception of the world, by its nature, demands such a clash. It describes the individual in a head-on confrontation with those forces that are striving to destroy the natural cycle of existence in order to give it a finished and rational harmony. Unless these forces are central to the author's vision and directly intervene in the fate of a particular individual no denunciations or grotesque distortions will produce the necessary artistic result.

It is tempting to accept the impression that the single main concern of the anti-utopian novel is to paint a picture of an undesirable future. Of course it is impossible to conceive of an anti-utopia that lacks such a vision. Yet none of the outstanding works in this genre *(We, Chevengur, Brave New World* or 1984) are simply a form of sociological prediction decorated with elements of narrative interest. They are instead a quite special type of fictional literature.

We have yet to fully understand the genre as an artistic whole but certain aspects are already clear today. The anti-utopian novel always depicts a violent attack on history: it is simplified and subdued and in the name of a dry and lifeless ideal there is an attempt to correct it. The hero is fated to experience this violence as the drama of his own life. For him at least this drama occurs once and for all, though it may be quite typical, pre-ordained and irreversible according to the logic of the Single State. Finally, this violence against history is also directed against nature, in the broad meaning of that term. The environment, the reasonable relations between man and the surrounding universe, and human nature are all under attack.

The anti-utopian novel, and this is its real vocation, shows us the world in the instant just before the last hour of nature has come. The individual therefore faces a moral choice as soon as he or she becomes aware that the final hour is very close.

For Zamyatin's D-503 the moment of choice came when he discovered that he possessed such an atavistic relic as a soul. Aldous Huxley also acted as Zamyatin's successor in this direction and a similar clash unfolds in his book. From our point of view this continuity is more important than the obvious parallels between the Single State and Huxley's depiction of the Age of Our Ford.

When *Brave New World* first appeared in 1932 it was chiefly understood as a satire aimed at a quite specific target. The author was thought to be mocking the dream of those who believed that intensive industrial mass production had brought an earthly paradise very close to hand. A worldwide economic crisis was raging and the frivolous dream of imminent paradise soon evaporated of its own accord. Huxley, it seemed, was merely marking the onset of sober realisation.

Soon, however, the pretexts for seeking such topical comment in the novel disappeared and its deeper meaning was uncovered. The clearest concern was an anxiety about the standardisation and amoral philistinism of contemporary society. These were not a passing epidemic for the author but the standard of the age. And he was not mistaken. The declared fundamental principles of his "brave new world" were commonality, identity and stability and proved a model for the joyless features of an age given over to the ecstatic pursuit of consumption. After Huxley's death in 1963 his book, which had been thoroughly forgotten, was remembered and seen as prophetic.

However, this is also a superficial interpretation. Serious literary criticism did not accept such a reading of the novel. This would have been right had there not been critical attempts to deny the importance of the book altogether. It was an essay not a work of fiction, some said, a subjective view rather than a penetrating insight into genuine problems. The writer and critic John Wain upbraided Huxley for sacrificing his profession as a writer to indulge in "tracts against materialism". It is also strange to read this today. The modern world is faced by quite different dangers because it has still not overcome hunger, illiteracy and poor living conditions.[11]

The dominant opinion today is that Huxley wrote "novels of ideas" and these only became genuine works of fiction when the main philosophical issue was properly concealed. This was not at all the case with *Brave New World* and so the book was placed on the lowest scale of values and easily ignored by those who wrote about Huxley. It was not considered a novel and the "idea" that was reduced to "materialism" was easy to refute.

Yet was "materialism" the main point here? Was Huxley's leading idea so straightforward?

To answer these questions we must first acknowledge that this is indeed a novel and not a sermon, and it evolves through a confrontation that is constructed according to the canons of art. Antagonistic principles each represented by their heroes come into conflict though we may admit that the protagonists are not shown as fully rounded personalities. There is, furthermore, the clash between these incompatible strivings as they unfold in the thinking of the book's main figure.

If the importance of this conflict is not appreciated then judgements about Huxley's novel will inevitably be sketchy, incomplete and essentially incorrect. The various interpretations of *Brave New World* that concentrate on distinguishing its central "idea" treat it as though it were a philosophical work and not a piece of fiction. They only show how naive it is to discuss anti-utopian works without appreciating that they are indeed fiction.

Huxley himself indicated the key to the central confrontation of his novel in the book's very first pages. The Central London Hatchery and Conditioning Centre or H.C.C. is being described. Genetic engineering helps to obtain excellent human individuals of different kinds. A Mr. Henry Foster who works at the H.C.C. describes its work and tirelessly proves its practical importance. Indeed the whole social structure is concerned: here society's needs in unskilled labour, rocket engineers and statesmen are all met by manipulating the post-natal development of thousands of embryos. The right results in the desired quantities and of the highest quality are assured.

These, however, are mundane and everyday productive activities. There are also higher aims that are not comprehensible to everyone although the results, if successful, will affect them all. These are to shift from mere slavish imitation of nature to the much more attractive world of human inventiveness. The substitution of these homunculi for children was only one point in this programme. And it embraced everything: there was not an activity or phenomenon under the sun it did not include.

After this Henry Foster is never again the focus of the story. There is no need: the most important words have been pronounced and the conflict unleashed. Moreover, the parable or anti-utopia is offered almost optimal artistic means for resolving this type of conflict. Everything that happens in Huxley's novel expresses in a variety of forms and projects how such a transition from "imitation" to "invention" may be implemented. Even in birth and death. Not to mention relatively minor aspects.

Culture, for instance, is rejected because it is considered unnecessary lumber. History is, to use Ford's famous word, "bunk". The past is blown up by dynamite placed under monuments while old books are destroyed. Suffering, weakness, courage and nobility— all are abolished and handed over to the College of Emotional Engineering. There they lose most of their similarity to the original meanings of these words; they bear as much resemblance to them as the bottled infants of the Hatchery do to a real human baby.

Under the onslaught of "inventiveness" the entire harmony and proportion of life's natural cycle, with all its rhythms and colours, is devastated ,to its very foundations. Everything is done to shift the emphasis "from truth and beauty to comfort and happiness. Mass production demanded the shift."[12] A "brave new world" is born in which the "fictions" called souls are dispensed with once and for all.

Is the world Huxley constructed so parochial in its spatial and temporal limits? Can we interpret the pictures flashing past the reader exclusively as a challenge to "materialism" and so on? It is possible. But only at the expense of their fuller meaning. And only if we refuse to acknowledge that the "final catastrophe" shown by Huxley and the logic that leads directly to this result is not restricted to a specific society. It does not just apply, in fact, to the society Huxley himself knew or the time in which he lived.

More than 50 years after the book's first appearance this should now be clear. There have been enough cases to convince us that the urge to "invent" rather than "imitate" has determined a great many of the features of our age. This is not a passion but a sinister tendency. It may take various forms but the results are devastatingly the same: it matters little whether we are referring to the triumph of sameness and ugliness or more specific examples (the Soviet "projects of the century" such as the diversion of the north-flowing Russian and Siberian rivers, that caused protests of the Soviet public).

Huxley had already described such a model state before. Scougan a character in *Crome Yellow,* describes a Rational State with its Herd and Directing Intelligences and examining psychologists who sort out the infants in order to determine for all time their place in the system. Published in 1921, this first novel was completed when Zamyatin was finishing writing *We*. This was the germ, then enriched by Zamyatin's influence, that eventually grew into *Brave New World.* Or so some suggest. Yet in *Crome Yellow* a figure like Bernard would be inconceivable, while in *Brave New World* he occupies the central place precisely at the moment when Huxley decided to create his anti-utopia. It was Bernard, after all, who focused within himself the main confrontation in the book. He was an enthusiastic supporter of the "brave new world" who then gradually came to realise he was its prisoner. A supporter of Order and Stability, he became an outcast when he began to experience feelings that the system could not control: hurt, fear, and a heretical irreverence towards the universally accepted codes of behaviour.

This awakening is even more significant and weighty than the dispute between His Fordship Mustapha Mond and the Savage, brought to London from another human era. They debate whether such a society is reasonable and the Savage constantly quotes from Shakespeare in reply. This persistent refrain, beginning with the title itself, is too obvious for the reader, however, and the quotations do nothing to counter the ideal of identity. It is a direct and didactic presentation of the author's position rather than a debate between equals. It is not hard to spot the source of this imbalance. It was too important for Huxley to present a line of thought that he had already long before developed. The task was assigned to the Savage.

There was no need to guess what the author thought of this "brave new world". He employed satiric hyperbole rather than forthright declaration. The satire illuminated the drama awaiting each individual who failed to dissolve his or her personality in the unanimity, mutual exploitation and other irreproachable principles of the "most progressive" of all progressive societies. At one and the same time, he could not free himself from its principles and hence remained its mournful captive.

As literary experience in the composition of such works accumulated it became obvious that it was not enough in an anti-utopian novel to know about the society. Knowledge of the individual who found himself faced by such a familiar and typically 20th-century situation of choice was also necessary. Choice was morally necessary although the circumstances were almost impossibly difficult. The nature of the choice might ceaselessly change from one novel to the next. So might the forms in which the choice took shape and the conflicts created by that choice. The necessity of choice remained, however. After reading Zamyatin and Huxley we can confidently say that this was an unalterable requirement of the genre. They were not consciously directed by the demands of the genre, of course: it had only just come into being. Most probably its founders did not have any idea of its future evolution.

* * *

Neither did they know that in 1929 when the campaign against Zamyatin was in full swing and Huxley had begun to write *Brave New World,* a work that would become a Russian classic of the genre was submitted for publication. Platonov's *Chevengur* was rejected, however, because of its "incorrect" portrayal of the revolution.

Even when set beside Zamyatin and Huxley *Chevengur is* an exceptional anti-utopian work. They were preoccupied by the knowledge of what might happen if already existing and rapidly growing dangers were not averted. Platonov instead had in mind the actual state of the world. His grotesque distortions belong, in Bakhtin's terminology, to the uncompleted present and not to the future that is far off but discernible. The "distant ideal" is always present in the utopian narrative but in Platonov is brought to within a very short distance of the present. He described a society where only the sun appointed to be the "world proletariat" will work. Yet the announcement of the instruction to establish such a system does not occur in the realms of fantasy but in a provincial Russian region only recently scorched by the receding lightning flashes of the Civil War.

This immediately also affects the nature of the clashes described and the choice of figures, among whom there are no personifications—a quite impossible occurrence in Platonov's world. Instead it all grows out of the upturned reality of the first post-revolutionary years. Having purified life of all "oppressive elements", the urge to build the road to communism with a single sweep of the hand, and make a break with the "mysteries of time" was no flight of the imagination but a widespread desire. As another of Platonov's heroes, Kondrov in "For Future Use", puts it, people then wanted to become "cleverer than reason". The Bolshevik characters in *Chevengur* like Chepurny, Kopenkin and others retain too much of this elemental fury and impatience for renewal to fit into a parable with generalised and easily identified prototypes. It is not hard to detect in each of them the imprint of the social psychology of the time the novel is describing. It begins with a laconic but expressive touch, that makes us sense the period: Dvanov visits the revkom (revolutionary committee) where the chairman tells him that "revolution is a risky business—if it doesn't work out we'll strip off the topsoil and leave only clay. .. " .

But the "topsoil" does not want to be carved up in accordance with the plans of those seeking such a "risk". The main clash in *Chevengur* arises from the quite stubborn resistance this "risk" encounters, though it may seem the resistance is feeble and anaemically manifested.

Sonya, the teenage girl Dvanov met before setting out for Chevengur, told him that one of their course teachers said "we are stinking pastry but he will make a tasty pie of us". Yet another formula typical of that period's attitudes: the Chevengur reformers were inspired by just such ideas about the common people and their own mission. It is demanded that "by summer even the grass should reveal our socialism!" and to ensure this, they wreck the foundations, with never a doubt that this might distort the path "to the communism of life". Revolutionary intuition is recognised as a reliable guarantee of the truth. It stirs them to mix the "pastry" with irrepressible energy and sweep aside as a kulak heresy any doubt as to whether the result will be edible. Yet the doubt still remains all the same. It arouses in Dvanov "the grief of unexpected danger". Platonov made Dvanov his central figure because he was the only one who was able to sense the truth as he listened to the other side, and he did not hastily attribute their arguments to the stale perversity of the peasant mentality. The main conflict in the novel is fought out in his soul.

Dvanov has already firmly mastered the fact, it seems, that "revolution is a violent thing and a force of nature". Nevertheless, he can grasp the "anxiety of the poor villages" and he recognises in the revolution itself "some kind of vanity ... higher than its young intelligence". He doesn't know how to refute the blacksmith's accusation: "You shoot first and ask afterwards ... you take away our grain down to the last ear of corn ... the peasant is left with nothing but the bare horizon." However many proofs he may offer that these confiscations are the "vital life's blood of the revolution" there's no way he can change Nedodelanny's conviction that since they've decided to destroy the economy "no one will have anything bigger than a chicken in five-years time". Neither does he refute the advice of Yakov Titych. The latter simply doubts in the necessity of communism since "all our long life will pass" without him and suggests: "You give a thought to the individual!" However, unlike Chepurny, he clearly understands that this is not a "proletarian thought " .

Such thoughts present difficulties for a mind awakened by the revolution but not yet very strong. Chepurny and Kopenkin's utopian initiatives are themselves most often only a way of avoiding reflections that could shake their faith. Platonov knew how devastating the consequences of an excessively revolutionary enthusiasm could be. In the Chevengur experiments, however, he perceived other much more malevolent threats. Alongside Chepurny there hovers the figure of Prokofy who cleverly reasons that communism should be portioned out only as far as it is expedient. You can't do enough for everyone, he argues: "Today he demands property, tomorrow a wife, and then happiness 24 hours a day... It will be better to gradually reduce the individual. He'll put up with it: he's going to suffer in any case." Yet another figure inevitably appears in Chevengur, the semi-literate Piusya who heads the secret police cell. He made reprisals against the class enemy "universal and public". The agricultural labourers themselves were to kill these enemies, at his command, thereby learning revolutionary justice without any gesture to the "black magic of thought and writing."[13]

When he was already working on *Chevengur* Platonov wrote and published an essay called "Che-Che-O" (1928) together with Boris Pilnyak. An important work in many respects, it refers to the acquired habit of looking "only from above" without acknowledging that the nation is made up of people "each one cleverer than the other". The glance "from above" does not distinguish individual features but only the human mass on which experiments can without hindrance be made: the bullying logic of an officer determines what is necessary and what harmful for the mass.

In spite of their poor origins both Piusya and Prokofy look at things "from above". Their concern is to "organise others" for a purpose that is inaccessible to the limited reason of those "others". Piusya and Prokofy do not doubt for a moment, naturally, that their goal is a noble one. Piusya "was getting ready to kill all the inhabitants of Chevengur", using the most effective means so as to inculcate in the "others" their obligation to help him in the most practical fashion because that was what was needed to thwart the intrigues of the hostile class. When he states his approval of the "purging of the city for proletarian settlement" Prokofy's passion for theoretical profundity leads him still further. He has already drawn up a plan of such an organisation of the town that would permit "a lot of excess to be confiscated from the individual". For example, only one should think while the others "live like empty wagons,"[14] follow instructions and carry no burdens.

It is not hard to recognise the circumstances under which such ideas could flourish. They required some support from the particular state of society created by that period. However, they also needed a particular way of looking at the world and in *Chevengur* the author gives more than hint at this. The inhabitants of Chevengur are in constant readiness for the end of the world. Just as typical is their reverence for the sun: it will abolish labour as a survival of the greed which facilitates unequal possessions and, hence, oppression.

Both are birth marks of the utopian perception of the world. They are already to be found in the millenarian faiths of the early Middle Ages. The Second Coming, the Day of Judgement and the subsequent harmony which would occur on earth, not beyond the grave. When Campanella described his ideal city he was able to draw on fragments of mythological and folk themes that depicted the sun as the king of the universe and earthly kings as solar divinities. Seen in the context of this pre-history, Chevengur is a reminder of the tradition of seeking for paradise on earth. Everything that happens in the town is a test of the very possibility of making utopia a reality.

All the same, there is still a popular belief that Platonov himself was a utopian. They suggest that *Chevengur* (and also the *Juvenile Sea* and "For Future Use") was a type of utopia.

If this view is accepted it is easy to discuss Platonov as a "romantic of the revolution" who extolled the "energy of life's renewal". But this is too one-sided a reading. It will hardly bring us any closer to understanding his works, probably the reverse.

Such interpretations are only possible, in all likelihood, when we become carried away by the fantastic aspects of his narrative and seriously believe that the society Platonov outlined was quite "arbitrary". Yet the world he describes is pervaded throughout by the roar of reality in which everything was shifted and disordered by the recent historical cataclysm. Platonov was writing about possibility which had now appeared for "popular truth to be actually put into practice on earth". He described the new stimulus that had been given to "traditional Russian historical 'truth-seeking'" in these conditions. We may say that this was his major theme here. To develop it he had to grasp all the complexity involved in this active "expectation of the truth of life", not in an abstract form but in specific matters suited to the present.

Naturally Platonov did not reject the idea of truth-seeking itself. He was criticising the hot-headed and blind methods by which it was put into practice. The human individual could not be treated as material for the construction of the earthly paradise, Platonov objected, even if its planners were inspired by no less than the triumph over death, of which they dream in Chevengur. A humanist of the Russian persuasion, Platonov could not agree to a golden age that demanded such devastating infringements of the "substance of life": all of the brief chronicle of Chevengur is marked by scenes where the innocent are punished and children die. He saw more in the Chevengur experiment than simply an outburst of anarchist enthusiasm that could not tolerate the drawn-out and lengthy historical process. It was more than the degeneration of impassioned romanticism into tyrannical cruelty. Here he discerned the real difficulties that accompanied the re-organisation of life according to principles of truth and justice.

The view "from above" increasingly became the norm and was ever more contemptuous of the masses. This was one source of difficulty. Another was the intolerance that took possession of the "masses" themselves and pushed figures like Kopenkin, Chepurny and Dvanov into the foreground. A certain adolescent maximalism made them contemptuous even of conversations concerning "the consistently advancing transitional stages". This was also in the spirit of the time. The dream of utopian thinking had to be immediately transformed into visible form: "and once Chevengur gives a ready model it will already be easy to make communism in all of our sixth part of the world".

This utopia was thwarted by the laws of reality. It was then violently introduced and with apparent success overcame "unreliable ... impassable nature"—the phrase describes the triumph of the Bubble, the Straw and the Bast Shoe in a fairy-tale recalled by Dvanov after the total liquidation of the Chevengur bourgeoisie as a class. It had only become easier to implement this "model" because the utopian perception of the world had been rooted in the "masses" with a proven reliability. After all, Piusya organises that eternal bliss for the bourgeois for which they had been prepared from their cradle upward, "on the basis of their own superstition" about the imminence of end of the world. As the near future would show, Platonov's utopians were not entirely wrong when they supposed that "this would be kinder" or else "all the common people would die in the transitional stages" to communism. *Chevengur* was completed on the eve of collectivisation. Very little time remained until the 1933 famine.

Did Platonov foresee such a course of events? It is difficult to doubt that he did, and not only because he next wrote "For Future Use" and *The Foundation Pit*. In *Chevengur* the advancing future is already quite clearly described: "all the doors were open because the houses were empty" and the inhabitants were happy to meet new people "because all they could acquire in place of belongings were friends."[15] The fields were left unworked so as not to create harmful objects that could increase the petty-bourgeois heritage. To ensure its final ruin subbotniks [days of unpaid labour.—*Tr.*] were organised during which houses were shifted and orchards dragged to other places. Utopia had been completed but "life rejected this spot and went off to die in thickets of the steppe".

Platonov reminded us that history is already loaded with tragedy but if we try to speed it up the tragic element sharply increases. Great dreams may inspire this impatience but thoughtlessly disregard the deformations that life itself undergoes in such a rush to transform.

* * *

Platonov's satire touches on a malevolent and vast subject. Today we use the terms "feudal" or "barracks" socialism to describe the Stalinist distortion of the revolutionary spirit. Both Soviet history and the worldwide prestige of socialism suffered a tremendous loss because of these distortions.

George Orwell's novels, particularly 1984, seem a natural continuation of certain themes in *Chevengur* although the English writer did not know Platonov's work. An English version first appeared in 1972 while Orwell died in 1950. Like Platonov's his achievement was also only recognised years later. In his lifetime he was valued for his sharp intelligence and gifts as a polemicist. No one then would have dreamed, however, of calling him a master of prose. English criticism in the 1940s was not afflicted by an artistic short-sightedness that was then suddenly corrected. Once again it was simply that an anti-utopian work had to prove its relevance to art as well as to politics.

Participation in the Spanish Civil War became the decisive turning-point in Orwell's biography. He fought for the Republicans near Barcelona where he was wounded. Then by a miracle he escaped arrest in purges that adopted all the methods already legitimated in the Soviet Union by Stalin's police chief Yezhov. Orwell, who until then had published under his real name of Eric Blair, went to Spain a convinced socialist. On his return he retained his faith in socialism as the only possible way to preserve humanity from the evils and afflictions brought by the 20th century. But a categorical hatred of enforced unanimity had now been added to his views. He detested the permitted lawlessness and terror justified by higher strategic and political necessity, i.e. all that was the inseparable essence of Stalinism. While not rejecting socialism he made a substantial qualification when defining his position: he was for democratic socialism as opposed to the totalitarian and Stalinist model. After Spain his works were devoted to the exposure and denunciation of the totalitarian idea and all its practical applications.

In 1940, Orwell wrote that for many of his fellow Englishmen "purges, secret police, summary executions, imprisonment without trial, etc., etc., are too remote to be terrifying. They can swallow totalitarianism *because* they have no experience of anything except liberalism."[16] Such passivity became the constant subject of his criticism. In return Orwell was either boycotted or ignored as if what he was saying was no more than the usual exchange between conservatives and radicals in the press. The subjects of Oceania, the state described in 1984, are under constant and vigilant surveillance. Nothing must escape the eye of "Big Brother". Yet there is no fear of subversive activity: it has long ago been excluded. The regime's higher goal is to not permit any deviation from the established order, including the personal and private life where such infringements have not yet been entirely eliminated in spite of the elaborate system of surveillance.

The individual must belong entirely to the regime, from head to foot, from cradle to grave. Crimes are not committed by those who intend to resist the state—such people simply do not exist. It is those who dream of not participating, though only for themselves and e ~ then out of work hours, who are criminal. Not only must there be no hint of intellectual freedom, even unrestrained feeling and the triumph of instinct are forbidden.

The totalitarian idea was intended to encompass in every sense all that made up the universe of human existence. Only then could it achieve its final goal. There would arise a "world of glass and concrete, unimaginable machinery and unheard-of means of execution". A nation of "warriors and fanatics bound together in an indissoluble unity" would be born "in order to move eternally forwards, inspired by completely identical thoughts, yelling completely identical slogans. Working, fighting, triumphing and forestalling: 300 million people with completely identical faces."[17]

In Orwell's work this is not the passionate daydream of a reformer inspired by a crackpot idea. With quite insignificant exceptions this is already a reality. The world is divided between three empires engaged in endless colonial wars. An enervated badly dressed mob flows along the street past dilapidated houses which smell of cabbage cooked in rancid oil and blocked drains. The majesty of Oceania in no way denotes the well-being of its ordinary citizens. They only have duties but no rights, and their first duty is unlimited loyalty to the regime. Not from fear but from a faith that has been made their second nature.

The paradox is that such sincerity is obtained by force and there are no provisions restricting the latter's application. The central problem of all those that interested Orwell lies here. How far, he asked, was force really able to turn the individual not merely into a slave but into a totally convinced supporter of the regime that was repressing him? "A boot stamping on a face for ever?" Where did compulsion end and conviction and rapture begin? Orwell thought that the enigma of totalitarianism lay in its ability to attain this effect, moreover on a mass scale and not just in isolated cases.

The solution lay, he believed, in the universal pervasiveness of fear. As it gradually became the most powerful of impulses, fear broke down the individual's moral rectitude and made him or her suppress all feeling apart from that of self-preservation.

To this end the regime took a number of measures that formed a strictly consistent logic. There was an exceptionally pervasive and effective surveillance. There existed the Thought Police and the Morals Police. Then there was a punitive system of unlimited capacities working in close cooperation with the propaganda system that daily engaged in brain-washing. Yet even all of this was in itself insufficient to attain total anonymity. Therefore particular methods of influencing the empire's subjects were invented, for example, the destruction of language. The regime needed an impoverished language. One word only for each thought and with a strictly fixed meaning, for all time ensuring the unilinear nature of the concept it symbolised. The main concern of the Ministry of Truth became "history": it had to put into practice the doctrine of the "moveable past". This said that the past was that which suited the present needs of the regime.

The ulterior aim here is understandable. History, culture and human nature itself were only obstacles and irritations that prevented the totalitarian idea from being implemented to the full. So long as even a feeble shoot of unofficial thought and civil feeling continued to grow neither "Big Brother's" despotism or the dictatorship of his "Party" as a whole could be considered immortal. It was not a question of finding opponents for they were not genuine anyway. The very possibility of disagreement had to disappear, even if it was thoroughly theoretical, ephemeral or incapable of finding political expression. Even as an abstract conception any type of individuality had to disappear once and for all.

There can be no doubt that Orwell had in mind the Stalinist system and its potential further evolution when he was describing Oceania. However, his subject was wider than that and concerned the illness that had taken different forms in different countries but nevertheless remained the same however much externals might vary. This affliction methodically strengthens the state by destroying the individual. It can be the power of a "Big Brother" whose face stares down from thousands of posters and portraits or that of an anonymous bureaucracy. One version is Stalinism, another the doctrine of racial and national superiority. A third is the complex of ideas guiding an aggressive technocracy that dreams of turning all into robots. The world Orwell described to his readers could actually take a great many different external forms. Any one of them, nevertheless, presupposes the insignificance of the individual and the absolute power of the state. The authorities rely on ideological conceptions that supposedly always infallibly guide them to the truth. No dialogues are therefore admitted.

The individual personality must be transformed, in the logic of this system, into nothing; he or she becomes a "bolt" or the dust in the camps, even when formally retaining liberty. Under no circumstances, moreover, can the state be satisfied with the might it has attained. Continually it must strengthen and increase its powers for that is the law of its existence. After all, it creates nothing apart from slavery and fear and admits no values or interests other than its own while portraying itself as the triumph of reason, justice and democracy.

This idea has traced many paths across the 20th century and become the foundation of those utopias that proved, on creation, to be nightmares. Orwell showed a society where this had happened and it is recognisable as a model that has had not a few imitators and copies. Once again it was shown that the anti-utopia helps our historical self-cognition and this is impossible where the outlines of reality are eroded (not invented but genuine), and deformed to suit the author's viewpoint. The classic utopia from More to Wells was born of theory. The modern anti-utopia is born of our own experience.

Yet this has not changed the laws of the genre. They require generalisation when specific detail is not enough, even under the magnifying glass of hyperbole. The novelist must grasp the principles and innermost thought that summons such Single States, "brave new worlds", and Oceanias into being. The "intoxication of power", an Orwell character calls it: the deifying of the boot under which shivers a bloody mass, what was once a human face belonging to a unique and irreplaceable individual. If we want to understand the meaning of this century's most terrible dramas this is probably not the full answer. But it is an essential part of the answer.

Another law of the genre, already intuitively discovered by Zamyatin, was adopted by Orwell as a matter of course. The serious anti-utopia is not fatalistic nor does it alarm us like the numerous depictions of a nuclear Armageddon in recent years. The world of the anti-utopia is always at the very brink beyond which begins the "last hour of nature". Nevertheless, there remains an alternative offered by the attempt to resist even when it seems in objective terms to be pointless. Most often this is not resistance to the system but merely an attempt to remain outside the system in private and unaffected spheres. There that same nature which is being mercilessly crushed for the sake of unswerving expediency has left its perhaps now hardly recognisable impression.

If we look at this clash with the pre-Orwellian anti-utopias in mind, it turns out that it is quite crucial, no matter how petty and mundane the details. The antagonists in this conflict are oppression and resistance, appeals to capitulation and riot, and the powerful will of the regime, on the one hand, and on the other, is the wounded, always concealing itself and mutely shy, but still not destroyed humanness. Before Orwell no one exposed the essence of this conflict so unambiguously.

The final denouement of this parable is easy to foresee and, of course, it is not the most important statement of the book. The hero does not hold out, is broken and returns from the cells a model representative of a nation of fanatics. Any other conclusion would have contradicted the entire spirit of the book. It is the inevitability that conflicts will arise which is most important here, although the regime has done everything to eliminate the very possibility of them. However grim the thoughts that visited Orwell concerning the totalitarian future awaiting the human race, he believed that forces of resistance would be found. The individual cannot be so enslaved that he or she really becomes only a cipher and renounces human nature.

1984 has also become a classic because it is illuminated by this hope.

* * *

Paul Tillich, who elaborated the doctrine of "theology of culture" considering Christian being as a chance to overcome social alienation, wrote a striking work entitled "Critique and Justification of Utopia". He stated in it that no utopia in its aspirations towards self-justification could become an entirely closed society. Its claims would also be proved false when it ignored the finite, such as history and earthly realities, instead soaring heedlessly towards its ideal no matter what it might be.[18]

The theological context of this statement naturally does not prevent it being true in other circumstances as well. The entire experience of the anti-utopia in the 20th century merely confirms his statement. Discussion will continue for a long while, probably, as to whether the genre has said all it has to say in artistic terms. There can be little doubt, though, that the range of problems such novels focus on has been of acute relevance throughout this century. In a sense the past 100 years have been an uninterrupted quest for a utopia capable of standing up to the tests of history. Hence so many of the false dawns succeeded by metaphysical disappointment that mark these years; hence so many of the convulsions, delusions and catastrophes.

The anti-utopia did not conceptualise this social and inner moral quest in its own distinctive way only to fall under the power of a mystical denial itself. No, its aim was to reject myths, point out the dead-ends, and ease their avoidance and transcendence. In this respect the anti-utopian novel has fully earned its praise.

NOTES

[1] N. Frye, "Varieties of Literary Utopias", *Utopias and Utopian Thought,* ed. by F. E. Manuel, London, 1973, p. 29.

[2] *Znamya,* No. 4, 1988, p. 128.

[3] *Literaturnoye obozreniye,* No. 2, 1988, p. 107.

[4] A. 1. Herzen, *Works* in 9 Vols., Vol. 7, Moscow, 1958, p. 181 (in Russian).

[5] *Znamya,* No. 4, 1988, p. 131.

[6] *Znamya,* No. 5, 1988, p. 114.

[7] Ibid.. p. 105.

[8] Ibid., p. 146.

[9] *The Collected Essays. Journalism and Letters of George Orwell. In Front of Your Nose, 1945-1950, Vol.* 4, New York, 1968, p. 75.

[10] *Znamya,* No. 5, 1988, p. 154.

[11] *Aldous Huxley. A Collection of Critical Essays,* ed. by R. E. Kuehn, Prentice-Hall, 1974, pp. 27-28.

[12] A. Huxley, *Brave New World*, New York-London, 1946, p. 273.

[13] A. Platonov, "Chevengur", *Druzhba narodov*, No. 3, 1988, pp. 97, 104, 128, 142, 143, 127; No. 4, 1988, pp. 58, 83.

[14] *Druzhba narodov*, No. 4, 1988, pp. 119, 69, 120, 69, 70, 120.

[15] Ibid., pp. 69, 75, 70, 69, 122, 83.

[16] G. Orwell, *Selected Essays*, London-Tonbridge, 1960, p. 36.

[17] *Novy mir*, No. 2, 1989, p. 160.

[18] *Utopias and Utopian Thought*, p. 308.

THE GUIDING IDEA OF ART

Nikolai Anastasyev[*]

The 1520s saw a heated polemics between Reformation leader Martin Luther and renowned writer and thinker Erasmus of Rotterdam. Erasmus responded to the German monk's challenge with his *De libero arbitrio,* and Luther, in his turn, made public his thesis *De servo arbitrio.* No matter how violent Luther might have been and no matter what exquisite causticity permeated his adversary's remarks, both defended the truth (certainly, each had its own concept of it), rather than his personal ambition.

In his time, Jonathan Swift deemed critical attacks on his contemporary Daniel Defoe insufficient and wrote *Gulliver's Travels,* conceived as a refutation of Defoe's *Robinson Crusoe*—imagination against earthly verisimilitude.

Without doubt, Erasmus and Luther were ideological adversaries. One glorified man's independence, the other proceeded from religious dogmas which excluded any attempt to analyse the Scriptures from the viewpoint of reason. It is as true that Swift and Defoe opposed each other not only artistically, but ideologically as well: scepticism against optimism. Yet, underlying the profound differences between them was their similarity. It was not by accident that they said in the 15th century that Luther hatched the egg Erasmus had laid. And it was not by chance that, while mocking Enlighteners' complacency and blind faith in reason, Swift used to say that he sincerely loved Johnes, Peter, Thomas and others. Defoe shared his feeling.

Humanism was their ideological commonality. A whole number of Soviet and foreign scholars (especially Alexei Losev) studied the spiritual dualism, even pluralism of the Renaissance as the cradle of the humanistic vision of the world. It proved to be astonishingly viable and ideologically attractive. Contem-

---

[*] **N. Annstasyev, D. Sc.** (Philol.), literary critic. Author of the books: *Faulkner. An Outline of Creative Work; Creative Work* of *Ernest Hemingway Renovation* of *Traditions. 20th-Century Realism in Juxtaposition to Modernism* and of a number of articles on 20th-century US literature.

poraries and compatriots argued with each other, same as representatives of changing epochs and nations separated by state boundaries. A precipice of difference lies between Michelangelo and Delacroix, Boccacio and Leo Tolstoy. This is a difference between the all-absorbing faith in progress that emerged at the dawn of capitalism, and the 19th century that witnessed cataclysms which largely enfeebled this faith. Yet the tradition was not disrupted, and the past, no matter how violently attacked, remained a living thing. The concept of man's attaining spiritual integrity (even in ideal) only through fraternity with others remained intact and was best expressed by Leo Tolstoy whose works marked the end of a whole age of artistic development. Here is a memorable episode from *War and Peace:* "Davout lifted his eyes and looked intently at Pierre. For several seconds they looked at one another, and that look saved Pierre. In that glance, apart from all circumstances of warfare and of judgement, human relations arose between these two men. Both of them in that one instant were vaguely aware of an immense number of different things, and knew that they were both children of humanity, that they were brothers."[1] Hegel wrote: " *The content is* nothing more than a *transition of the form* into the content, and *the form is* nothing more than a *transition of the content* into the form."[2] This idea, as any other, may certainly be vulgarised by trying to find out pedantically whether certain themes, characters and plots fit into this or that system of artistic representation. Yet, liberally interpreted, it helps trace and explain the most important laws in the development of art.

The more intensively social and ethnic stratification of the human community proceeded, the more visibly inner relations between people and the individual and the community weakened. At the same time, people's mentality for a long time retained its reliance on the universal interconnection of everything, the natural order of things which saves man from loneliness by involving man into itself.

In general, this feeling predetermines the form of modern European literature. Naturalness and harmony of proportions characterise the artistic world, be it Defoe's verisimilitude or Gogol's grotesques. This structural harmony testifies to the integrity of the humanised cosmos. Formal alterations make it easier to judge about changes in art in the 20th century.

Lukach maintained that "the progressive realistic line almost disappears with Cezanne and van Gogh."[3] If we do not engage in polemics over what representational realism is and what its historical modifications were, it must be acknowledged that the scholar precisely dated the end of the realistic tradition, ousted by Picasso's horribly distorted figures, Malevich's geometry, and Rauschenberg's collages. In other words, self-professed constructivism replaced the natural image. The role of technique was augmented, which is especially evident in avant-guarde art, be it painting, literature, music, or theatre. Yet, even where continuity is preserved and classical experience is perceived as an intrinsic value, the nature of style is evidently changed. The direction of efforts is reversed: formerly, literature did its best to get rid of its conventionality, whereas now it splurges it. Thomas Mann considered Goethe a supreme manifestation of genius, yet, *Wilhelm Meister's* natural and easy narrative style is alien to him. The author of *Der Zauberberg* orchestrates the action, keeping the reader aware of his presence all the time. Max Frisch and Kurth Vonnegut went even further, whereas William Faulkner avoids displaying his presence anywhere, with Yoknapatawpha County nonetheless being a glaringly artificial world.

This exaggerated geometry of the form and-style sometimes finds a simplistic explanation: the authors cannot write and so substitute philosophising for art and an illusion of literature for genuine literature. As I see it, such arguments hold no water.

Let's compare the above quoted episode from *War and Peace* with the following one from Hemingway's *A Farewell to Arms:* "We were quite awhile and did not talk. Catherine was sitting on the bed and I was looking at her, but we did not touch each other. We were apart as when someone comes into a room and people are self-conscious."[4]

Such are the extremes: two enemies knew that "they were brothers", and two lovers that "they were apart".

A mere several dozens of years caused the building which had been erected for centuries to crumble.

Alexander Blok called this a collapse of humanism: "We have lost the harmony between man and nature, life and art, science and music, civilisation and culture...."[5]

In his report of 1926, Thomas Mann called this an end of "Lubeck as a form of spiritual life". We...are witnessing the end of an age, the bourgeois-humanistic and liberal age which started with the Renaissance and reached its peak with the French Revolution, and we are now witnessing the last spasms of its agony," Mann wrote in his article *Coethe and Tolstoy. Fragments for the Problem of* Humanism.[6]

"*The form is* nothing more than a *transition of the content* into the form."

Modern style which has lost the former harmony reflects a quite different perception of the Universe and the changed status of man in Cosmos.

Contemporary literature's protagonists float in vacuum, no circumstances binding them to anybody or anything; they are loners dragging their injured wings behind them, separate people, as Hemingway would have called them, *steppenwolves,* as Hesse would have said. Kafka was more categorical, and even cruelly naturalistic: "No one can be sure of anything, therefore one can say nothing. One can only shout, stutter, wheeze. The conveyer of life is carring man somewhere—nobody knows exactly where. Man turns into a thing, an object, ceasing to be a living creature."[7] We saw how it happens in his story "Metamorphosis". Even Faulkner's characters, endowed with the knowledge of their roots, fall into hollow emptiness: "...there was something definitely rootless about him, as though no town not city was his, no street, no walls, no square of earth his home."[8]

"In our days, everything seems pregnant with its contrary," Marx said over a century ago.[9] Nowadays, his prophesy became a reality captured in art. As the fundamentals of humanism are destroyed, genre conventions are turned upside down. A utopia was still possible in the late 19th century, and Edward Bellamy wrote his *Bachward 2000-1887.* The first anti-utopia, Evgeny Zamyatin's *We,* appeared 30 years later, followed by Aldous Huxley's *Brave New World,* William Golding's *Lord of the Flies,* George Orwell's *1984,* and Kurth Vonnegut's *Slaughterhouse Five, or the Children's Crusade.*

In 1925, Ortega-y-Gasset wrote his famous essay *The Dehumanisation of Art,* often viewed as a manifesto of art for art's sake. Indeed, it stated clearly that "the new art obviously addresses itself not to everybody, as did Romanticism, but to a specially gifted minority."[10] Arrogant as it may seem, this statement in fact merely notes linguistic changes. Previously, artists were deeply interested in the real world and human life, whereas now "the preoccupation with the human content of the work is in principle incompatible with aesthetic enjoyment proper". "Even though pure art may be impossible, there doubtless can prevail a tendency toward a purification of art. Such a tendency would effect a progressive elimination of the human, all too human, elements predominant in romantic and naturalistic production."[11]

One has a double impression from Ortega's logics. He asks essential questions: "Whence the dehumanisation of art? Whence this aversion towards living forms?" He says: "Should that enthusiasm for pure art be but a mask which conceals surfeit with art and hatred for it? But, how can such a thing come about? Hatred of art is unlikely to develop as an isolated phenomenon; it goes hand in hand with hatred of science, hatred of State, hatred, in sum, of civilisation as a whole. Is it conceivable that modern Western man bears a rankling grudge against his own historical essence? Does he feel something akin to the *odium professionis* of mediaeval monks—after long years of monastic discipline—against the very rules which had shaped their lives?

Yet at the last moment Ortega seems to take fright at the depths he had looked in and evades the answer: "This is a moment prudently to lay down one's pen and let a flock of questions take off on their winged course."[12]

Say what you will, but the Spanish philosopher and aesthete made a remarkable insight into modern art. He did not sermonise or lecture, he grasped the essence of characteristic changes and laboriously analysed them. The loss of roots in the external world led to the reduction of the individual part in the personality's spiritual and intellectual composition. Man was gradually ousted from the centre to the suburbs of the microcosm, merging with others until no longer discernible, losing his own views and habits, and finally, his name, which became an utter convention.

In this sense, the emergence of the "new novel" was not a paradox, but a rule, and its anti-aesthetics was not an entirely new thing. True, "new novelists" opposed themselves to their forerunners, for instance, Kafka and existentialists. But what did they object to? To the evasiveness and lack of consistency of *The Trial's* author, and Camus' and Sartre's attempt to add a human touch to their works, even in absurdity disguise. The characters retain their names, although somewhat clipped, and are given at least some freedom of action. In general, they are quite lively, which is undesirable. If one declares man's metamorphosis into an inanimate object, one has to be consistent to the end. If fact, Robbe-Grillet is: his characters are fully dispersed in the inanimate world.

Such is the limit of the dehumanisation of art.

* * *

The potential of spiritual sanity, accumulated over the centuries of humanity's existence, cannot be wasted in a flash. After all, artists did not intend to imitate impassive chronologists of the West' decline. The entire history of the 20th-century art is an agonising quest for a new point of support.

Since the outside world had become a hostile force which subverted, rather than protected individuality, it was natural to turn to lonely spirits, able to endure this pressure from outside. This shift became apparent already with Joseph Conrad whom many of the 20th-century writers considered their precursor.

Both Conrad and Hemingway are often called humanists, but the traditional perception of humanistic writers implies that "they all almost live and pursue their activities in the midst of the contemporary movements, in the practical struggle; they take sides and join in the fight, one by speaking and writing, another with the sword, many with both. Hence the fullness and force of character that makes them complete men."[13]

Now, what about Lord Jim and Frederic Henry, or characters of Proust, Aldington, Hesse and Nabokov—are they social people? Do they belong to any party? On the contrary, they can fully display their capacities only in conditions of a "separate world". If there is any link between them, then it is generation affinity.

The best of them are distinguished for their great personal courage and noble morality; that is why they managed to survive in time retaining their charm and ability to influence people. But one cannot live as an escapist all the time.

Along with other things, loneliness as a way of thinking can breed self-destroying egomania. Literature makes this very graphic as well. For instance, intellectuals Saul Below and Iris Murdoch lost self-discipline and self-control and only sigh in a boring manner about their personal disadjustment to the world. Certainly, much depends on the author's idiosyncrasies. Ironical estrangement as a form of criticism is one thing, and sympathetic or even neutral contemplation is quite another. Observers are not happy with, say, modern French literature. This is what a recent article says about it: "The author's maniacal assertion of his individuality averts the smart reader. Instead of creating his own world and invite everyone else there, the writer is preoccupied only with his own uniqueness. Since now, he no longer informs, but confesses all the time. All these voices of loners, speaking about their petty griefs, create a universe of total alienation where everybody talks about himself and never bothers to hear others out."[14]

The tragedy's transformation into a farce is a long process. One can well expect highly original books to appear and bring back a lonely voice of a man who does not want to adopt conventional cliches and dissolve in the faceless crowd.

Yet, it has transpired long ago that individualism as a moral value is unable to compensate for the lost ideals. Andrei Platonov wrote a propos *A Farewell to Arms:* "Love quickly devours itself and stops altogether if lovers avoid including certain non-love, prosaic facts of reality into their feeling; if it is impossible or undesirable to combine a passion with participation in a cause pursued by most people". Another excerpt from the same article says: "The involvement of Henry and Catherine into... the common life could have imparted to their happiness depth, constantly renewable freshness and inexhaustible immortality, as they would have been then nurtured and supported by the whole world, rather than a couple of frightened, semi-childish and trembling hearts."[15]

As is known, Hemingway preserved his love for his early characters and advanced towards the very same "common life".

Stefan Zweig was one of those writers who were very much distressed about the collapse of humanism. He swayed between gloomy despair and radiant hopes for the better, and eventually took his life, unable to tolerate this dualism any longer. Seven years before his suicide, Zweig wrote a novelistic biography of Erasmus which revealed the same confusion of feelings. He starts it by saying that Erasmus, "the luminary and glory of this century", is lost in oblivion now, and ends in the following way: "Let cold intellectuals prove mathematically that Erasmus' idea has no future, and let reality seems to confirm their righteousness again and again; still we will always need individuals who in the midst of conflicts will remind us about what nations have in common and who revive a dream of humanism's triumph is human hearts". But what was in the way of "fruitful insanity" of the early humanists? Zweig gives the following answer: "Like the

Germans invaded Ancient Rome, fanatic Luther invaded their super-national dreams and along with him came irresistible forces of the national popular movement."[16] The opposition of national aspirations and supra-national dreams and a supra-national language (Latin) becomes the recurrent, and, eventually, the key theme in the book.

Historically, Zweig is wrong: it can be repeated once again that Luther was as much a humanist as Erasmus, only he enveloped their common idea into more pragmatic forms. Erasmus represented the intellectual elite—a republic of scholars, and the Reformation leader relied on the grass-roots. Obviously, Zweig looked at the 16th century through the prism of modern ideas and delusions, which is not a rare thing to occur. And nowadays, as everybody knows, there are heated debates about national identities and cultures. One can even say that the national idea emerged as an alternative to the humanistic idea.

However, this opposition has not always been clearly perceived. Thomas Mann's *Betrachtungen eines unpolitischen* which openly emphasise a national idea verging on chauvinism are, according to their author, the reflections of a humanist. Anatole France and Theodore Dreiser also took nationalistic stands during the First World War and they as well did not think that they betrayed the spiritual legacy of the past.

Sometimes, ideas became polarised (true, it was later and in absolutely different conditions). The movement for political independence in Africa gave rise to the Negritude theory and art which were overtly opposed to the European, i.e. humanistic, tradition. Negro folklore, purified from the latest cultural con-tamination, was offered as the only source for this concept.

Similar things underlied the American "black literature" concept which appeared during the upsurge of the civil rights movements in the USA.

Certainly, historical reasons amplifying the national idea in art may be different. In any case, though, culture which narcissically studies its own reflec-tion and prefers soliloquy to any other form of expression is doomed to decline. Goethe understood this 150 years ago and said: "National literature is of little significance nowadays; it's the turn of an international literature, and everybody must promote its quick advent."[17]

True, such daring revelations came easier at that time, as the feeling of the universal interconnection was still there, and any attempts to disrupt it by stressing one's personal uniqueness were considered to be bold encroachments on humanism. Associating himself with Samuel Johnson, Leo Tolstoy said that pa-triotism was the last refuge of villains. But in the 20th century as well, tempted by mirages of national self-sufficiency, literature sooner or later became aware of the futility of this route.

Rebelling against the pestilential atmosphere of chauvinism, which set in Germany during the First World War, Hesse recalled his great countryman's words: "He placed love for humanity above love for Germany, and he knew and loved it as no one else did. Goethe was a citizen and patriot in the international world of thought, inner freedom and intellectual conscience; and at his best moments he soared to such heights as to perceive nations' destinies in their subordination to the world's whole, rather than in their isolation."[18]

Faulkner developed a reputation of a committed American from the South, but he used to say that if the spirit of nationalism takes root in literature, the latter ceases to be itself. Problems the artist takes up and which are worth writing about, devoting music to them or painting them—these are problems of the human heart having nothing in common with race identity, the colour of the skin. In his view, national distinctions and relations are not only important, but are dangerous if paid too much attention. People must remain first and foremost human, he said.[19]

He stated this in the mid-1950s, when America, caught up in the euphoria of its postwar affluence, once again became convinced of its Messianism.

Can there be more orthodox patriots in the sense of attitudes towards a cultural legacy and national roots than Latin Americans? Nonetheless, Carpentier is equally interested to discuss Creole mythology and European intellectual tradition, from Pascal to Sartre. In his view, "nativism" has little originality, and folklore is important and necessary only to the extent to which it "connects us with *eternal universal categories.*"[20] Peruvian prose writer Roa Bastos uses the term "cosmovision" to define the specificity of modern Latin American novel.

Certainly, declarations are only declarations, but they become rooted in art. Faulkner's Jokpanatawpha cycle explores the roots to the same extent as the overcoming of the roots. Garcia Marquez' novels contain severe national self-criticism. *The Patriarch's Autumn* shows how the abject dependence on tradition and ritual turns a nation into an obedient crowd. Macondo owes all its troubles to the fact that it is an island which egocentrically isolated itself from the rest of the world.

Great Britain presents an absolutely different literary tradition, but raises the same issues. Take one of the most impressive postwar novels, *Daniel Martin* by John Fowles. The main character, homonymous to the novel, is an intellectual writer engaged in a hectic quest for such spiritual integrity as would at least resemble that of his predecessors. Yet, he fails: the world of arts is corrupt with the rat race for glory and money; the world of politics is ruled by militant all-goes attitudes; and the generation gap became a yawning abyss. The character flees to the country to think there about his roots, about "Englishness"—in a vain hope that rural England has retained real life but, alas, local exotica proves to be absolutely unable to oppose faceless post-industrial civilisation. As the narration reaches its finale, this idea becomes more pronounced. Looking at Rembrandt's

Self-Portrait in a London art gallery, Daniel becomes keenly aware of the noth-
ingness of his time, himself and his art.

* * *

It would be appropriate to talk now about what is currently being discussed in this country, as these discussions are more than nationally significant.

Fifteen years ago, French personalist philosopher Jean Marie Domenach
published an essay *Modern Culture: An Attack on Human*ism. Among his opponents were "new novelists" and representatives of the latest theoretical trends, all
convinced that "man is dead".

The publication did not receive much attention as its central idea became
a commonplace already at that time. There would be no point in referring to it
now if similar ideas were not developed in this country as well. Some of our
authors also attack humanism, although from a different angle.

At the round table of the *Inostrannaya literatura* magazine devote to the
centennial of Fyodor Dostoyevsky's death, literary critic Vadim Kozhinov said
that almost all Dostoyevsky's writings have an anti-humanist edge (taking humanism in its preceding meaning). This kind of humanism is addressed to the individual rather than personality, if only because humanism presupposes a certain
object of humanistic treatment and the personality cannot be treated as an object.
Another participant in the round table, Yuri Seleznyov said roughly the same
thing: "It is not the self-valeur of the personality— the central category of the
humanistic mentality—that determines his [Dostoyevsky's—N. A.] 'Cosmos', but
the notion of *the community.*"[21] In one of his subsequent articles, Seleznyov developed this idea comfortably to the whole classical Russian literature. What he
says is that the latter's national specificity is based on the delineation of its national character and the humanistic ideal of a free and independent individual.

Such is his idea. I have to recognise that it does not hold water historically speaking, for it proceeds from a false assumption that humanism in its
original sense is equal to individualism. If we agree to this, we have to dismiss
Thomas More from the humanistic tradition, as his Utopians were connected to
each other by firm moral and practical obligations. Besides, John Donne, who did
not share the Renaissance optimism, but was close to the humanistic understanding of the world and individual, wrote that no man could exist by himself as an
island. As for the personality as an "object of treatment", Hamlet would hardly
acknowledge himself to be one.

Nonetheless, this idea struck a resonant chord with some people who
drew, so to speak, practical conclusions from it, which boiled down to the following: the national character of Russian and Soviet literature is their characteristic

feature as distinct from "cold internationalism" inherent to the West. This national character has to be carefully preserved, they insist.

In his article "Talking to the Reader", literary critic Vladimir Bondarenko says, in particular: "Unlike other nationalities, it has for a long time been considered improper for the Russians to talk about their identity. Is not this why unbridled *Russophobia is* rampant now in the press?"[22]

For a numerically small nation, it is natural to emphasise its identity, especially if it is threatened with complete assimilation. But whence this inferiority complex with representatives of a great nation ?

I referred to Bondarenko's article, because it expresses a crucial need for a "unifying idea". It is saddening, though, that the critic erodes this idea by his reasoning.

Bondarenko is doubtless right in distinguishing "national" from "nationalistic". Yet, he obviously fails to understand that the fine line between them may easily disappear if national consciousness is focused only on its uniqueness. There is no artist without roots—this is axiomatic. Yet, equally axiomatic is the idea that the foliage, at least cultural, is nurtured not by the roots alone. Meantime, the article says a lot about national languages and national types of people, and never mentions a cultural dialogue. As a result, the national character, this integrating factor, is actually being equated with the roots.

Let us take a closer look at Bondarenko's line of thought. He quotes his opponent of long standing, literary critic Natalya Ivanova as saying: "... if one a priori applies a caste approach to one's culture, one should in the first place try to look at this problem form the point of view of another nation...". Bondarenko comments: "it goes from bad to worse. In other words, to understand what Russian novel is, one has to adopt the vision of, say, a Chinese critic."[23] To be honest, I do not see any reasons for irony here. Perhaps, it would be useful to read a Chinese critic as well; besides, it has long become a commonplace that Russian novel developed in close creative interaction with European novel and so can be understood only in the general aesthetic context. Can one fully appreciate Tolstoy's discoveries without comparing *War and Peace* to *La Chartreuse de Parme?* Apparently not. In any case, Tolstoy openly recognised the lessons literature had learned from Stendhal. On the other hand, can we appraise Hemingway's books without measuring them by Tolstoy's yardsticks? Apparently not. In any case, Hemingway constantly held in his mind the Russian classic's epoch-making experience (and openly admitted doing so, too), and it does not matter that it did not become an ultimate criterion for the author of *A Farewell to Arms*.

To put it in other words, not unifying idea can evolve out of national specificity.

Yet we must acknowledge that the critic sets the right task. There is hope that with time we may find reasonable solutions. Regrettably, the edifice of European and world culture is too often divided into mutually impenetrable sections for "ours" and "theirs".

* * *

The Russian Revolution of 1917 gave rise to great hopes. Many perceived it as a living alternative to the seemingly dead past.

Recalling the years when "the world was much closer to revolution than it is now, Hemingway recovers a feeling he lived with in his youth: "In those days we who believed in it looked for it at any time, expected it, hoped for it—for it was the logical thing."[24]

Are these lost illusions that are behind the tired scepticism of *Fiesta* and especially *A Farewell to Arms?*

Unwilling to give up the classical legacy of thought and spirit, Thomas Mann, for one, dreamed of an union of old and new values: "Socialism... would never raise to the implementation of its truly national task unless Karl Marx reads Holderlin; this encounter seems to take place soon."[25]

Rolland, Dreiser, Barbusse, Malraux harboured similar hopes.

The initial enthusiasm was so great that even the most intelligent and shrewd people did not want to admit that the promises given to the Russian and other peoples in 1917 were gradually forgotten, and that the revolution turned into its opposite. At the peak of the Great Terror in Russian, Lion Feuchtwanger wrote his notorious *Moscow* 1937.

Yet, hopes gradually faded away to be replaced by disappointment which was not always openly expressed. Andre Gide published his famous *Le Retours de l'U.R.S.S.;* as for Rolland, Brecht, and Becher, they did not publish their diaries as they believed that any criticism of the Soviet Union would hamper the anti-fascist front's unity. Now, as we gradually get familiarised with them, it becomes perfectly clear that it is unjust and unworthy to lay all the responsibility for Stalin's personality cult on the world intellectual community the way Vadim Kozhinov did (cf. *Nash sovremennik,* No. 4, 1988).

Historians argue whether there was an alternative to the Molotov-Ribbentrope Pact of 1939. Maybe, this polemics will bring us closer to the truth. What is indisputable is that the pact shocked the world intellectual community and averted many of the Soviet Union's former sympathisers.

That was an open falloff. And what was behind doubts confided only to notebooks? The answer is: the Stalin regime's crimes, only a smaller part of which were then on the surface.

Yet, I think that was not the most important thing. It turned out that "proletarian humanism" in Stalin's interpretation was not only against a union with Holderlin, but sought to humiliate him. The notion of personality was cast off as unnecessary, therefore an issue of the individuals's independent participation in life lost all significance.

I am aware that Arthur Koestler's novel *Darkness at Noon,* which was written 50 years ago, but reached our reader only now, evoked controversial feeling with many people. It is understandable. Lenin's associate Nikolai Bukharin has just been rehabilitated. From publications of his articles, his widow Anna Larina's memoirs, from his brilliant biography by American historian Stephen Cohen, Bukharin emerges as a highly moral person who remained a daring thinker both in his revelations and delusions. And all of a sudden, a book appears with Bukharin as a protagonist of the main character who is far from a wholesome and morally perfect person. Certainly, the novel emphasises that he was a victim to the ruling regime, but the inner logic of the narration leaves no room for doubts that Nikolai Rubashov, a former minister and popular hero, deserved his lot. He is guilty of having betrayed his honesty and conscience, and not what they accuse him of.

So, if one reads *Darkness at Noon* as a novelistic biography, one may disagree with the author about his representation of Bukharin's personality.

But such an approach will lead us astray, even if we take into consideration the author's note that Rubashov combined the features of not only Bukharin, but Trotsky and even Radek as well. What we witness is not a drama of a historical personality or an invented hero, but a drama of an idea whose executors, including the main one, are of secondary importance. This is an intellectual novel belonging to German, rather than English, tradition, and its style is the least interesting thing. The most important thing is the depiction of a mode of thinking which tests and refutes itself to finally obtain lucidity of thought—alas, illusory and suicidal one.

During the investigation, Rubashov argues with an interrogator who presents a composite image, rather than a specific person named Ivanov. His mentality reflects the general way of thinking which subjugates the hero to its implacable logic.

"For the movement was without scruples; she rolled towards her goal unconcernedly and deposed the corpses of the drowned in the windings of her course. Her course had many twists and windings; such was the law of her being. The motives of the individual did not matter to her. His conscience did not matter to her, neither did she care what went on in his head and his heart."[26] This is Rubashov's inner monologue.

"... a conscience renders one as unfit for the revolution as a double chin. Conscience eats through the brain like a cancer, until the whole of the grey matter is devoured... Sympathy, conscience, disgust, despair, repentance, and atonement are for us repellent debauchery.... History is a priori amoral; it has no conscience.... There are only two conceptions of human ethics, and they are at opposite poles. One of them is Christian and humane, declares the individual to be sacrosanct, and asserts that the rules of arithmetic are not to be applied to human units. The other starts from the basic principle that a collective aim justifies all means, and not only allows, but demands that the individual should in every way be subordinated and sacrificed to the community..."[27] These fragments of Ivanov's monologue echo Rubashov's line of thought.

Rubashov's another interlocutor, a prisoner from the next cell, has no name whatsoever: he is simply No. 402. Indeed, does he need a name? His words about decency and honesty he transmits to Rubashov with the help of a prison code convey unbearable pangs of conscience of the revolutionary himself who was suddenly lost in the intricacies of the I-We relations. Rubashov removes the ensuing emotional tension by an effort of will: "What was decency? A certain form of convention, still bound by the traditions and rules of the knightly jousts. The new conception of honour should be formulated differently: to serve without vanity and unto the last consequence."[28]

This is Rubashov's tragic delusion. It would be more precise to call it a tragic transformation of an idea; man was supposed to move from the realm of necessity to the realm of freedom, whereas in actual fact, he became just a cog in the state wheel.

Artistically, Koestler's novel lends itself to criticism. The sufferings of thought are alleviated there; doubts too quickly suppress dialectics.

Yet, let us admit that Arthur Koestler laid special emphasis on the issues which have concerned everybody throughout the entire 20th century, notably, the destiny of humanism, its real forms and deformations, its deadlocks and prospects.

Let's take a step back, to an epoch when voices of people who still believed in old values weaved themselves into prophesies of universal decline. Gilbert Keith Chesterton wrote mediocre novels and excellent detective short stories. He displayed his capacities to the full in his essays in which he employed his extraordinary spiritual energy to combat with what he termed as "contemporary homeless scepticism".

"In truth, the story of what was called by Optimism was rather odd: When I had been for some time in these, the darkest depths of the contemporary pessimism, I had a strong inward impulse to revolt; to dislodge this incubus or throw off this nightmare. But as was still thinking the thing out by myself, with little help from philosophy and no real help from religion, I invented a rudimentary and makeshift mystical theory of my own. It was substantially this: that even mere existence, reduced to its most primary limits, was extraordinary enough to be exciting. Even if the very daylight were a dream, it was a day-dream; it was not a nightmare. The mere fact that one could wave one's arms and legs about (or those dubious eternal objects in the landscape which were called one's arms and legs) showed that it had not the mere paralysis of a nightmare. Or of it was a nightmare, it was an enjoyable nightmare."[29]

Chesterton wrote this in 1936, shortly before his death, the time when a similar perception of the world was exceedingly rare. He seemed to be a person who regained paradise on earth, Kafka noted about Chesterton many years ago.

Chesterton's naive optimism was unexcelled. On the other hand, however, literature in general reappraised its former values as well. Thomas Mann expressed the reasons of change in the following statement: "Hitler had a special quality: he simplified human feelings evoking staunch 'no', clear and deadly hatred. The years of anti-Hitler effort were a morally benign age."[30]

A real threat loomed over culture, notably, the idea of national superiority which assumed extreme, ugly, criminal forms in nazi Germany. In these conditions, the humanistic idea was revived, and its historical potential and absolute value stood in the way of noxious Hitlerism .

What was the most important thing about *Josef und seine Bruder* was, according to its author, the humanisation of myth, which, naturally, called for a revision of this notion. Josef is a novel of the soul, which runs contrary to the original mythological tradition. The composite image of the Biblical hero, as Thomas Mann presents him, is at the same endowed with a powerful and self-conscious individuality. "Human ego's ambitions to present itself as the centre of the Universe are prerequisites for the discovery of God, and the inspiration of ego's lofty mission is originally connected with the inspiration of humanity's lofty mission."[31]

In this period, Hemingway was also engaged in the quest for harmony between the individual and the community—the foundation of humanism. Certainly, Robert Jordan is spiritually linked with the characters of Hemingway's earlier books, but at the same time what helps survive is not his personal perseverance alone. We witness the development of his ties with the same "common life" Platonov spoke about.

Like *For Whom the Bell Tolls,* Mikhail Sholokhov's *And Quiet Flows the Don* was completed in 1940. Here the seemingly lost sense of plentitude of life is also recovered: "And now that little thing for which Grigory had yearned through so many sleepless nights had come to pass. He stood at the gate of his own home, holding his son in his arms.

"This was all life had left to him, all that for a little longer gave him kinship with the earth and with the spacious world that lay glittering under the chilly sun."[32] A fragile attainment, which at the same time seems to be too much for a man who seemed to have lost everything.

Theodor Adorno's words that poetry is impossible after Auschwitz are well known. Apparently, it is impossible in its pre-Auschwitz form. The German philosopher was partly right: neo-avant guarde art, from the theatre of absurd to the "new novel", denies art in the sense of its emancipation from its human contents. Yet, the humanistic tradition rehabilitated in the prewar years persisted and sometimes assumed translucent, open, and, by virtue of this, simplified forms. Take, for instance, historical novels by Marguerite Yourcenar, Andre Maurois' prose writings and essays, or Thornton Wilder's novels one of which tells about the people of the Eighth Day, which has not yet come, but is sure to do so.

The most significant works of art are drifting away from gloomy pessimism and complacent rosy dreaming to study the dialectics of individual, tribal, class, and national relations. This is a point of coincidence for different writers and traditions. A character of Vassily Grossman's *Life and Fate* formulates a question which has been haunting the literature of the East and the West: "Tell me, what the might of an omniscient and omni-present creature will yield to the world, if this creature is left with our current animal self-assurance and egoism—class, race, state, and individual."[33]

In general, there are few books like Grossman's novel, and now this shortage is especially evident. One can even say that literature entered a period of a certain slowing down, and even Latin American novel today is no longer what it used to be. However, one should not fall into despair about this. Literature does not lose its energy and spirituality in such periods. When everything on earth, is closely intertwined, when we become increasingly aware of the global interdependence of nations, countries and cultures, humanism, perceived as a source of harmony between universal and class, global and national values, living humanism still remains the guiding idea of art.

NOTES

[1] Leo Tolstoy, *War and Peace,* New York, n. d., p. 905.

[2] G. W. F. Hegel, *Enzyklopadie der philosophischen Wissenschaften in Grundrisse,* Berlin, 1966, p. 135.

[3] G. Lukas, *Die Eigenarl des Aslhetischen, Vol.* 2, Berlin-Weimar, 1981, p. 740.

[4] E. Hemingway, *A Farewell to Arms,* Moscow, 1969, p. 134.

[5] A. Blok, *Collected Works,* in 6 vols., Vol. 4, Leningrad, 1982, p. 334 (in Russian).

[6] T. Mann, *Gesammelte Werke in Dreizehn Beindm, Vol. 10, Frankforl-on-the-Main,* 1974, pp. 165-166.

[7] G. Tallouch, *Gespradu mit Kafka,* Frankfort-on-the-Main, 1968, p. 160.

[8] W. Faulkner, *Light in August,* Harmonsworth, 1960, p. 25.

[9] K. Marx, F. Engles, *Collected Works,* Moscow, 1980, Vol. 14, p. 655.

[10] T. Ortega y-Gasset, *The Dehumanisation of Art,* Princeton, 1948, p. 6.

[11] Ibid., pp. 10, 12.

[12] Ibid., pp. 45-46.

[13] F. Engels, *Dialectics of Nature*, Moscow, 1964, p. 22.

[14] *Literaturnaya zhizn za rubezhom*, 1988, Issue 16, p. 33.

[15] A. Platonov, *The Crandeur of Simple Hearts*, Moscow, 1976, pp. 392, 393 (in Russian).

[16] S. Zweig, *Triumph und Tragik des Erasmus uon Rotterdam*, Berlin, 1986, pp. 9, 154, 84.

[17] J. P. Eckermann, *Gesprache mit Goethe in den letzten Jahren seines Lebens.*, Berlin, Weimar, 1982, p. 198.

[18] H. Hesse, *Gesammelte Werke, Vol.* 10, Frankfort-on-the-Main, 1970, pp. 414-415.

[19] W. Faulkner, *Articles, Speeches, Interviews and Letters*, Moscow, 1985, pp. 369, 387 (in Russian).

[20] *Latin American Writers on Literature*, Moscow, 1982, p. 37 (in Russian).

[21] *Inostrannaya literatura*, 1981, No. 1, pp. 199, 192.

[22] *Moskva*, 1988, No. 9, p. 183.

[23] Ibid., p. 184. 24.

[24] *By-Line: Ernest Hemingway*, London, 1970, p. 77.

[25] T. Mann, *Collected Works*, in 10 vols., Vol. 10, Moscow, 1961, p. 291 (in Russian).

[26] A. Koestler, *Darkness at Noon*, New York, 1956, p. 57.

[27] Ibid., p. 109.

[28] Ibid., p. 111.

[29] C. K. Chesterton, *Autobiography*, London, 1969, pp. 93-94.

[30] T. Mann, *CesGmmelte Werke, Vol.* 12, Berlin, 1956, p. 287.

[31] Ibid., p. 459.

[32] M. Sholokhov, *And Ouiet Flows the Don*, Moscow, 1964, Book 4, p. 861.

[33] *Oktyabr*, 1988, No. 4, p. 46.

THE MASTERING OF A NON-NATIVE LANGUAGE AS THE STUDY OF SIGN OPERATIONS

Revekka Frumkina,[*] and Anna Mostovaya[**]

The view has been current since time immemorial that nothing but good can come from learning a foreign language in addition to a person's native tongue which he can learn spontaneously in his parental home. The only debates on this score were centred on such issues as which language is more useful (or more prestigious, or more necessary, etc.) or what the preferred specific goals and methods of such study must be. We shall not tire the reader with proof of this: examples may be found both in various educational systems and in fiction.

In the Russian cultural tradition, enlightenment was always linked with openness to other cultures and languages. All the more paradoxical is the conviction that the study of a foreign language, particularly at a young age, is or may be harmful. Of all the possible harmful effects, the following are stressed: "the child's intellectual development may slow down, as may thinking in the native language and overall conceptual thinking; at times, the danger of speech disturbances arises; and so on."[1]

One of the consequences of inadequate teaching of a foreign language (called "uncontrolled inculcation of bilingualism" by the Estonian writer M. Hint) is believed to be what Hint calls, together with some other authors, "semi-lingualism" (see works by the Swedish linguist Nils Hansegard and his colleagues). According to Hint, semi-lingualism is a state of affairs in which a per-

[*] R. Frumkina, D. Sc. (Philol.), Professor. Specialist in psycholinguistics and semantics; author of many works in this field: Colour, *Meaning, Likeness; Semantics and Categorisation,* and others.

[**] A. Mostovaya, post-graduate at the Institute of the Russian Language, AS. Specialist in psycholinguistics and semantics. Author of many articles on the subject.

son supposedly command of two languages does not in fact have a command of either of them: coming up against a slightly more complex cognitive construction than usual, the speaker is unable to express it adequately in any of the languages of which he "has a command".

In the article quoted here, the non-native language the teaching of which may do harm and result in "semi-lingualism" is Russian. We can understand Hint's feelings, the more so that one of the authors of the present paper took part, some 30 years ago, in work on the methods of teaching Russian to Estonians.[2] It is immaterial, however, from the point of view of psycholinguistics and developmental psychology, what the specific non-native, foreign language is. If science indeed has what Hint refers to as "indubitable facts" it does not matter whether they point to the harm done by the early study of Russian, French, or Swedish.

Sharing the concern expressed by Hint, Vasil Bykov and other colleagues about the fate of national cultures and traditions, we intend to stay here within our professional competence, without encroaching on the sphere of social politics, especially on issues of inter-ethnic relations. We would like to steer, as much as we can, off problems of pure method, although some of them will have to be touched upon. There is one more preliminary remark we must make; the term "bilingualism" has always been somewhat fuzzy; at present, its meaning, in addition to being quite protean, is invested with a halo of social passions of extraordinary intensity. We therefore intentionally use this term in quotes, to indicate that it belongs to other authors. We ourselves speak only of the extent of mastery of a non-native language. We can now proceed to the matter in hand.

Semi-lingualism and semi-culture. Semi-lingualism is a very real phenomenon of our days, one that undoubtedly merits scientific analysis. Most "semi-linguals", however, are incapable of expressing a thought not because the situation demands that they should know two languages and they know none: as a rule, they have a fine command of their native language and have never seriously studied any other. Still, their verbal behaviour fully answers Hint's description. How is it to be explained? A hundred years of the development of cultural anthropology have shown conclusively that all languages adequately serve their cultures. A culture has nothing in it that could not be expressed in the language of that culture. However, when a certain cultural tradition is for some reason interrupted, a person finds himself immersed in "semi-culture"; its carriers become, accordingly, "semi-lingual" in the sense in which many authors, including Hint, use that term.

Mikhail Zoshchenko's heroes, the hero of Albert Camus' *The Stranger,* many of Vasily Shukshin's characters—they are all "semi-lingual". Only the direction of causality is here the reverse of what is implied by Hint and others: semi-culture is the cause and semi-lingualism, the effect, rather than vice versa. Semi-culture as we see it is not a lack of "culture in general", it is not a lack of knowledge. It is a situation of conflict in which a person finds himself as a result of breakdown of a cultural tradition. Any migrant is in this sense "semi-cultured": he who is pushed by the pressure of circumstance into the urban world and thus torn away from the established peasant way of life,[3] as well as he who chose to move from the world of ancient traditions and values to a highly civilised but not at all highly cultured environment (that is the situation of some individuals from the developing countries who come to study at European and American universities). Under favourable circumstances, this semi-culturedness is temporal, under unfavourable ones, it becomes a permanent factor.

The breakdown of a cultural tradition inevitably gives rise to a conflict of values. This places the individual into a situation of an extremely difficult choice, both social and personal. The tragedy of this choice largely colours the above-cited article by Hint. Science, however, must remain impartial. We must therefore reconsider Hint's idea that a "semi-lingual" individual is incapable of verbal expression of cognitive constructions of any degree of complexity.

Unfortunately, professional writers and public figures, not just ordinary speakers, are very inept at expressing cognitive constructions, not even very complex ones. We shall illustrate this generally acknowledged state of affairs by citing an example from an editorial text appearing in Literaturnaya *gazeta* (No. 3, 1989): "Of course, the questions, just as the answers, are of a personalist *(lichnostnyi),* subjective character" (the reference is to the readers' questions addressed to the writer Vasil Bykov and his answers to them.—*The Authors).* A question may be personal *(lichnyi),* not personalist, personality-oriented *Lichnostnyi);* an opinion or judgement may be subjective or personal; finally, an answer may express a personal opinion. But the phrase "a question (answer) has a subjective (personalist) character" is not normative in Russian.[***]

The fact that the standard of spoken and written Russian, especially of officials, is very low is common knowledge; besides, that is not our subject at all. But the *Literary Gazette* example is not as trivial as might seem at first sight. The reader will realise this after reading the sentence that follows the above-quoted one: "But the right to have, and express an opinion of one's own, is an inalienable feature of a democratic society". This context enables us to guess what "cognitive construction" the authors of the editorial text preceding the publication would have liked to express. What they had in mind is this, we believe. The questions addressed to Bykov reflect the views, interests, doubts, etc. of the readers; and the

---

[***] Much as the present translator hates to split hairs over an issue on which he fully agrees with the authors, it must be noted in all fairness that grammatically the word *lichnostnyi* in the Russian sentence is not connected with *vopros* "question" but with *kharakter* "character", which can certainly be *lichnostnyi* or *lichnyi* or any other kind, said word being just a general purpose prop in contemporary Russian. This, however, merely proves the authors' point as to the sorry state of Russian writing in this day and age—at the authors' expense.—*Tr.*

answers, the personal position of the writer Bykov rather than of the editors. Underlying a stylistic lapse is, we are inclined to believe, a definite value conflict that is new in our society: on the one hand, under *glasnost,* the editorial comments like the one we cited above are superfluous; on the other, the editors are accustomed to publishing only what they agree with, especially on large-scale social problems. The socio-cultural situation is a new one, and a standard linguistic instrument for controlling it has not yet been devised.

We can thus say that "semi-lingualism" is a real phenomenon of our society produced by "semi-culture". An interesting synchronic cross-section of "semi-lingualism" as a socio-cultural phenomenon may be obtained by generalising observations recorded in a normative dictionary[4] based on these data (see the description of "semantic devaluation" in Yuri Stepanov's work.[5]) Enough has been written on the factors which produced, and continue to produce, "semi-culture." We ought to read carefully, though, Lydia Ginzburg's observation pertaining to the 1920s: "In 1921, a certain professor publicly stated that what was happening in the country was a liquidation of literacy [the official phrase for combating illiteracy was the "liquidation of illiteracy."—*Tr.].* That is true in one sense and untrue in another. In actual fact, the number of illiterates in the direct sense decreased and the number of illiterates in the figurative sense increased."[6]

Early "Bilingualism" and Its Effect on Child Development. The controversy about the effect of early "bilingualism" on child development was acute enough already at the beginning of this century. Its intensity was proportionate to the acuteness of the socio-cultural conflicts in those communities in which one language in a poly-lingual population played, for certain historical reasons, the dominant role (Belgium, partly Switzerland, Canada, the USA). Both positions constantly figured in the literature of the question: the idea that any additional knowledge, including the knowledge of a second language, may only be useful, and the view that early "bilingualism" is harmful.

Let us try to find out how the assumption came into being that "bilingualism", especially early bilingualism can have a negative effect on child development? One of the first researchers to express, in 1915, the view on the harmfulness of early "bilingualism" was I. Epstein, a member of the associative school of psychology.[7] In simplified form, his line of reasoning could be presented as follows. Thinking is embodied in associations between concepts and words. If concept a corresponds to word *b* in one language and word c in another, the establishment of association *ab* may interfere with the establishment of association *ac.* When, however, the two associations *ab* and *ac* (corresponding to the "verbal equivalents" of concept *a* in two different languages) are established, both word *b* and word c suffer from interference in association with concept *a.* Interference is thus possible in the case of different words belonging to different languages and corresponding to a single concept. Hence the conclusion that early "bilingualism" interferes with the transmission of thoughts and even with their formation, inasmuch as language takes part in the formation of thought.

The assumption that bilingualism has a positive effect on the child's psyche and the prospect of his development apparently follows from some general ideas as to the mutual connections between language and thought. If language is an instrument of the conceptualisation of the world, two or several languages probably increase and expand the possibilities of the means of understanding the world, which partly coincide and partly differ from and complement each other. Those were the arguments used, in his polemics with I. Epstein, by W. Stern, a well known researcher in child speech. He believed differences between languages to be a powerful stimulus for individual acts of thought, for comparisons and delimitations, for the realisation of concepts within established limits, and for the clarification of the subtlest nuances of meaning.[8]

The 1920s marked the beginning of intense studies intended to establish experimentally the differences between mono- and bilingual individuals, and thus to determine the "vector" of the effect of early "bilingualism". The effect was studied of early "bilingualism" on such individual characteristics as (a) capacity for language learning; (b) level of mental development as a whole; (c) personality features. Let us briefly outline the results obtained in some of these studies.

(a) *The effect of bilingualism on the capacity for language learning.* The view that bilingualism has a positive effect on language learning is based on the natural assumption that a bilingual finds it easier to master a third language because he has a greater experience in language learning in general than monolingual individuals. The opposite view, however, was also current. The results obtained in this field were contradictory. In 1944, comparing the data on the progress of 69 bilingual freshmen with similar data on monolingual freshmen of the control group, D. T. Spoerl came to the conclusion that bilingual individuals showed somewhat better results in learning English.[9] On the other hand, some results were interpreted as confirming the opposite hypothesis. In 1935, N. Toussaint discovered that Flemish-French bilinguals in Belgium showed much poorer results at dictation-taking than monolinguals:[10] U. Weinreich believed that only further study could explain the discrepancy between these findings.[11] It is clear apriori, though, that success at dictation-taking is not exactly the best way to test the capacity for language learning: dictation-taking shows the degree of mastery of spelling rather than language the two things are distinctly different in any case, particularly in the case of individuals belonging to "non-bookish" culture.

(b) *The effect of bilingualism on the level of mental development.* One of the first experimental studies in this area was D. J. Saer's work *The effect of bilingualism on intelligence;*[12] in 1923, D. Saer tested 1,400 children in five rural and urban localities in Wales. The tests showed, first, higher results in urban children, both mono- and bilingual; second, better results in monolingual rural children (compared to bilinguals). According to Saer, the cause of this is that urban children have to resolve the conflict between Welsh and English at an early age, before entering school, while in rural children this conflict, interpreted as one between the individuals' "positive self-consciousness" and the "instinct to obey" comes to a head later, when they can no longer overcome it.

In 1928, E. Jamieson and P. Sandiford tested Canadian Indians; they discovered that in three areas out of four monolinguals were superior to bilinguals in intelligence levels.[13] Spoerl believed that her bilingual testees (college freshmen) did not differ from monolingual ones in the level of intelligence but were better at professional activities. To correlate these contradictory results of various experimental studies, S. Arsenian undertook in 1937 an overview of the field.[14] The considerable discrepancy between the results of various experimental studies were explained, in his view, by the drawbacks of the methods used in them. In his own study, Arsenian used a subtler set of methods distinguishing between different stages of bilingualism; he studied 1152 Italian and 1196 American-born Jewish children aged between nine and fourteen. The study did not indicate any significant influence of bilingualism on the level of intelligence within the group as a whole or within any of its parts. No correlations were discovered between bilingualism and school adjustment, either.[15]

(c) The effect of bilingualism on personality formation. Systematic study of the effect of bilingualism on personality formation was begun in the 1930s. As we know, "bilingualism" often develops in areas of contact of two or several cultures, which complicates the entire sociocultural situation. It may be assumed that the formation of the individual under these conditions is first and foremost affected by the non-triviality and complexity of the social environment as a whole. "Bilingualism" is only one element of this complexity and at the same time its most obvious reflection. It is easy to see, though, why special studies were often focused on the effect of "bilingualism", although the latter should more realistically be interpreted as a concomitant factor in the overall effect of the sociocultural situation on personality formation. The point is that "bilingualism" is directly observable, while the isolation of the principal factors in the totality of all that forms the "environment" is an incomparably more complex task.

The need to search for culturally conditioned causes of personality features (if there are any) of bilingual individuals was pointed out already by A. Weiss: he insisted that the individual's psychological integrity suffers from the complexity and instability of the external conditions of life rather than from a collision of linguistically consolidated conceptual systems.[16] Views were then expressed which were almost literally identical with what is now formulated by publicists and other writers. Thus in 1934 F. Sander wrote that "bilingualism" undermines personality structure, causing conflicts within the conceptual system.[17] In his opinion, "bilingualism" does not simply cause harmless slips of the tongue but goes much deeper, threatening the closed and self-concentrated integrity of the developing structure (especially, we believe, if it is forcibly inculcated at an early age).

Contemporary evaluations of the effect of early "bilingualism" on child development are on the whole more moderate and cautious. Thus N. Miller believes that the conviction concerning the difficulties of language learning in bilingual children is largely based on faulty methods of evaluation of the success of speech activity in general and of child speech activity in particular. His observations show that experts who are speakers of the language under study are inclined, in their judgements on speech activity, to regard all deviations from habitual norm (even such features as a slight specific accent) as retarded development of language competence.[18] In actual fact such "anomalies" may apparently affect the success of communication but they cannot be regarded at all as a sign of inadequate development of language competence.

K. C. Gardner considers factors like motivation and attitudes in the study of a second language.[19] In his opinion, the success of study and depth of assimilation of a second language is greatly affected by the individual's ideas as to just how pressing the need for learning a second language is, and whether it is difficult or easy.

Of Soviet studies in early child bilingualism the most. interesting ones are by N. V. Imedadze.[20] The following elements of his theory have the greatest relevance to the present study. Imedadze believes that the most favourable situation for the development of early bilingualism is the "one person one language" situation. Examples: the child speaks in French with his father and in German with his mother (see J. Ronjat's early data[21]); the child uses Russian in communication with nurse and grandmother, and Georgian, with mother and father; etc. The "one person one language" principle, i.e., the strict conditioning of the choice of the language of communication by the older participant in communication helps the child to realise the integral quality of the system of each language. In the final analysis, this principle facilitates the emergence of real bilingualism, eliminating situations in which two languages are mixed haphazardly in a single utterance.

However, even in situations in which the "one person one language" principle is always implemented in communication with the child, two stages in the child's speech development are clearly distinguishable, according to Imedadze. Stage one is the stage of language mixture: words belonging to two different languages, or repetition of equivalents of the same concept in two languages, are observed in the same statement; active interference of grammatical forms and constructions is also observed. Stage two is the stage of complete lexical and grammatical differentiation of two languages. Stages one and two are separated by a process of gradual differentiation of the language systems in question in the child's speech. As a result, towards the end of the second year of life such a differentiation of systems is achieved that the need to speak in one language completely excludes the other language.

Interestingly, semantically equivalent grammatical categories of the two languages are not always simultaneously mastered by the child in the process. One of the factors affecting earlier realisation of some grammatical category in one language compared to other languages (we refer to a grammatical category with the same semantics) is "perceptive distinctness" of the grammatical markers of the category in question. In his observations of Serbo-Croatian-Hungarian bilingualism, for instance, Mikes noticed that Hungarian locatives denoting spatial relations appear in the child's speech much earlier than locatives in the same child's Serbo-Croatian speech. In Hungarian, locatives are expressed in the form of affixes while in Serbo-Croatian, just as in other Slavic languages, through prepositions and case-endings. In his analysis of Mikes's observations, D. Slobin interpreted this difference as the effect of greater perceptive disctinctness of locative markers in Hunragian compared to Serbo-Croatian.[22] Earlier assimilation of some category in one language may, at least in principle, accelerate the assimilation of this category in another language. This type of interaction may be regarded as the effect of bilingualism on the child's cognitive development, and an apparently positive effect, at that.

A more general question, formulated by Imedadze, follows from the observations cited above: Does not child bilingualism facilitate an early awareness of the sign character of language? In other words, does not early bilingualism free the child from the idea that the object and the word denoting it are linked by an obligatory connection (from "nominal realism", to use Piaget's term?)

To test this hypothesis, Imedadze mounted an experiment involving 18 bilingual children of five and six with practical command of Russian and Georgian. In the experiment, the children were asked questions (in Georgian): "What is a name?", "Where is the sun's name?", "Does the sun know its name?", "How do we know the sun's name?", "Why do we call the sun the sun?", "Can we call the moon the sun and the sun the moon?" The experiment showed that bilingual children, just as monolingual ones, are not aware of the arbitrariness of the connection between the object and its name. Thus in response to the question "Where is the name of the sun?" (an improperly formulated question, in our view), the children replied: "In the sky, of course." In response to the question "Why do we call the sun the sun?", the children replied: "Because it shines." In response to the question "Can we call the moon the sun and the sun the moon?", the children replied: "If we call the moon the sun, it will become hot"; "No, we can't, it will not give light." Only one of the 18 children gave this answer in response to the question "Why do we call the sun the sun?": "Names are given by men." These results, Imedadze believes, point to the fact that early bilingualism does not in itself change anything in the object—name relation. Bilingual children give the same kind of answers which were recorded by Piaget in monolinguals. Under some conditions, though, early bilingualism may help the children to realise the sign character of language and the development of linguistic abilities, Imedadze believes. Bilingualism may become a condition of accelerated development of the arbitrariness and conscious character of speech where a child has to express, within limited time and space, one intention through equivalent means of two languages, i.e., to solve one communicative task by different means. The difficulties arising in this specific activity may ensure the development of an ability necessary for a conscious, controlled command of language. Only in this case, Imedadze believes, does a second language have a relevance to the general development of intelligence and to the development of linguistic thinking in particular.

Early Teaching of *a Non-Native Language as a Problem* of *Teaching Sign Operations.* In what follows we shall only be concerned with the situation of controlled teaching of a nonnative language, leaving aside the situation of the formation of natural bilingualism in mixed marriages, communication with coevals, etc. First, let us sum up the arguments "for" and "against" in present-day literature. Their comparison with the above over-view (in accordance with the tasks of the present article, the review deliberately left out all works on problems of language contacts, language interference, etc., including fundamental works of V. Rosentsveig, A. Shveitser, and others) indicates a lack of novelty in the position "for" as well as in the position "against". The *pros* are the plasticity of the child psyche, the child's ability to learn a non-native language by the way, as it were; the *contras* are the assumption of the competition between the native and the non-native language in the sphere of the incompletely formed cognitive automatisms and the concomitant hypothesis concerning the slowing down of the rate of general mental development.

Let us consider more closely the position "against". To substantiate it in practice, we would have to compare carefully the rate and quality of the development of the thinking (both verbal and non-verbal) of children some of whom studied a nonnative language in early age (e. g. beginning at four) and others did not. Let us note that any comparison of this sort is extremely difficult. The reasons for this, as pointed out by many researchers are extremely varied.

First, the tests of the level of mental development (used by the authors of the above-mentioned works) are unreliable in view of their orientation towards Europe-American culture of the urban variety. Second (and this is especially clear to educationalists who have to handle particularly difficult tasks, namely to teachers of special schools for children with physical and mental defects), any teaching experiment is unreliable as such. Both physical and mental development of children is highly individual: motivational factors closely interact with the influence of the family and the teacher's personality. Third, it is a well-known fact that the study, e.g., of French by English-speaking children encounters difficulties entirely different from those occurring in the learning of German by Russian-speaking children; the degree of generality of results obtained in different countries is therefore unclear. If we add to this the interaction of the factors (method of teaching X the teacher's personal qualities X the child's personality), it will be clear that all conclusions drawn from the results of teaching experiments can only be qualitative, and must by evaluated very cautiously.

It will be useful, however, to ask oneself if there are any apriori properly psycholinguistic, psychological or didactic considerations in modern science concerning the harmfulness of early teaching of a non-native language. Let us point out two assumptions, current in the literature, about the nature of man's innate ability to master speech: (1) we are born with an ability to master language *in general;* this does not depend on our ancestors' genotype; (2) we are born with an ability to master a language which is correlated with our ancestors' genotype, that is to say, we have abilities skewed towards the mastering of a definite language or languages. The present authors share the first viewpoint. As for the possible harm, we can only point out one apriori but extremely general consideration: early teaching not reinforced by proper motivation is absolutely harmful. This, however, is not a specific feature of the study of a non-native language only: just as harmful is, or may be, early teaching of any knowledge, if it implies oppression of the child's personality. On the contrary, to the extent the child can view the teaching situation as attractive, he will gladly add yet another game, the learning game, to the ones he already knows.

As for the general psychological and psycholinguistic arguments in favour of early teaching, it will be appropriate to begin with an analysis of early teaching of things which will seem at first sight extremely remote from the teaching of a non-native language. Our further argument will be based on the unpublished data of A. Zvonkin; conversations with A. Zvonkin helped to crystallise the conception evolved by the first of the present authors. [23-25]

For several years Zvonkin taught mathematics to children at the preschool age (four to six years). The content of those lessons was the study of certain extremely general relations between the objects of the real world, and also the discovery (mostly in visual terms) of certain general laws. For example, a four-year child has considerable difficulty in grasping the meaning of the relation between part and whole, the general and the particular, between set and subset. These words did not of course figure at the lessons. But if a child is shown cardboard figures with four angles, and if figures in which all the angles are right ones are singled out, and if, further, figures in which all the sides are equal are singled out among the right-angled ones (which the child can see for himself), after a while the child will not feel surprised at the fact that a square has three names: it is a square, because its sides are equal; it is a rectangle because its angles are right angles; and it is a quadrangle because these angles are four in number. At the same time the similarity between this task and the question whether fathers and grandfathers are men, and men are human beings, is established.

In another assignment, the children had to construct, with the aid of a mosaic game, sequences of a definite type out of partly-coloured chips (inserted in holes in the square field of the mosaic). The question arose of identifying the sequences which have already been constructed to avoid repetition, and to further construct, out of the given set of chips of different colours, *different* sequences of the given length. Supposing the child has chips of two colours- red and white. The idea that comes first is to draw circles, a red one and a white one. "But we do not have a white pencil," says the teacher. The child must somehow arrive at the idea that he can do without a white or a red pencil: the important thing is to have pencils of two different colours. In other words, a method must be found to designate the colour difference between the two chips. Generally speaking, this may be done not only by using a difference in colour. In this way the child is gradually led to the idea of denotation, of the reflection of a referent in terms of signs, and further, to the idea of the bilateral essence of the sign. Zvonkin gradually introduced semiotic ideas in the children's minds. The common element of two apples, two books, or two chips is their number. In all these cases we have two objects. But a book and an apple, a book and a pencil are also two objects. If it does not matter what these two objects are, if the only thing that matters is their number (children have to be told things like "Will there be enough pencils for all?"), there is a convenient mode of *designating* the fact: the figure 2. Or the Roman II. Or the word "two." Materially, these signs are different, but they mean one and the same thing. Similarly, if it is important to state that we have two different chips, a red one and a white one, it is not necessary to use the colours red and white: a red chip may be denoted by a square and a white one, by a circle. Two letters my be used. What letters? In the end the children guess, that the letters need not at all be *r* and *w* for *red* and *white.*

On the approach described here, Zvonkin taught children sign operations simultaneously showing them that the sign is arbitrary (the signifier is not connected with the *essence* of the signified), and that there is an isomorphism between the different systems of signification. The children become accustomed to the fact that numbers are designated by figures; sounds of speech, by letters; and musical sounds, by notes. They realise gradually that letter A and figure 1 may be written in different type and colour, and also transmitted by signal flags or the Morse code. From this, it is but one step to an understanding of the native of sign systems of all types: e.g. the sign system underlying geographical maps, and others.

What has been said here of the teaching of mathematics points to the supertask set by Zvonkin: instilling in the children the idea of semiotics as the science of signs. The same idea may be very naturally introduced in the early study of a non-native language.

The fact that a familiar object need not have a single name, that it may be called different names in different languages, systematically shows the child the difference between name and denotatum. It does not matter that tomorrow he may forget some of the new words: it is important that he should remember that such a situation is natural. It does not matter that the child will construct, in play, a fantastic plural in his native tongue on the analogy of a recently heard non-native plural. It is important that the child begins to understand that he can turn one cube into many by performing some simple operations on signs rather than objects. The fact that similar sounds of the native language may be designated by completely different letters is a great discovery for the child, provided he really understands the fact, not simply pretends to understand it. But this sort of discovery is usually made when the child is taught to write, that is, at school. However, even at four the child may easily absorb these "conventionalities" as meaningful if he understands that a letter is a sign, and that the main thing is not the learning of facts but acceptance of certain conventional rules similar to rules of games.

In the opinion of experienced teachers, the main shortcoming in the learning of a non-native language by small children is the situation in which children are not taught sign operations and given material for thought and hypotheses: instead, they are given badly structured information in the hope that the child's memory will work, and that the games method is automatically successful. Unfortunately, early (and not only early) teaching of a non-native language follows a schema like the one in the example which we borrow from Zvonkin's work "Children and Mathematics That Does not Look Like Mathematics." Let an adult be taught to count up to ten in Japanese: it*chi, ni, san, shi, to, roku, shiti, hati, ku, ju.* Supposing we learn this sequence. Now solve this task: Mother bought *ku* apples and gave *shi* children *ni* apples each. Question: how many apples has she left? A person who learns for a month this difficult science of counting up to *ju* has a fine mechanical memory. But a good mechanical memory has little to do with intellectual abilities; the main thing is that it serves nothing and develops nothing.

We are all born with a nearly unlimited potential for learning, for studying the diversity of the world. The human mode of effective processing of information is the structuring of diversity through identifying semantic invariants in it. This central idea, learning to identify the semantic invariant, may be easily assimilated by the child if he discovers that different means must be used in different languages to achieve the same goal (asking politely, thanking correctly, explaining where he lives, etc.).

If the teaching of a non-native language, be it Russian or English, at three or five, at the kindergarten or at school, is connected more with exercises in mechanical learning by heart rather than with the idea of meaningful invariants—that is obvious nonsense. But philologists, educationalists and writers will agree with us, we hope, that the study of any subject, and of anything at all, may be brought down to the level of learning to count up to *ju*.

NOTES

[1] M. Hint, "Bilingualism and internationalism", *Druzhba narodov*, No. 5,1988, p. 239.

[2] Ibidem.

[3] V. Bykov, "Nation. Language. Culture", *Druzhba narodov*, No. 6,1988.

[4] V. I. Vekurov, L. V. Rakhmanin, L. I. Rakhmanova, *A Short Dictionary of Difficulties in the Russian Language*, Moscow, 1968 (in Russian).

[5] Yu. S. Stepanov, "The European language union and European grammar today", *Inostrannaya literatura v shkole*, No. 3,1969.

[6] L. Ya. Ginzburg. "The choice of subject", *Neva*, No. 12,1988.

[7] I. Epstein, *La Pensee de la Polyglossie*, Paris, 1915.

[8] V, Stern, "Die Erlernung and Beherrschung fremder Sprachen", *Zeitschrift fur padagogische Psychologie*, No. 20,1919.

[9] D. T. Spoerl, "The Academic and Verbal Adjustment of College Age Bilingual Students", *Journal of Genetic Psychology*, No. 64,1944.

[10] N. Toussaint, *Bilinguisme et education*, Brussels, 1935.

[11] Weinreich, *Languages in Contact*, Paris, 1970.

[12] D. J. Saer, "The Effect of Bilingualism on Intelligence", *British Journal of* Psl~cho loy, No. 14, 1923.

[13] E. Jamieson, P. Sandiford, "The Mental Capacity of Southern Ontario Indians ", *Journal of Educational Ps~chology*, No. 19, 1928.

[14] S. Arsenian, *Bilingualism and Mental Development*, New York, 1937.

[15] R. Pintner, S. Arsenian, "The Relation of Bilingualism to Verbal Intelligence and Sch ool Adjustment", *Journal of Educational Ps~chology*, No. y1, 1937.

[16] A. Weiss, "Zweisprachigkeit und Sprachtheorie", *Auslandsdeutsche Volkforschung*, No. 1, 1937.

[17] F. Sander, "Seeliche Struktur und Sprache; Strukturpsychologische zum Zweispr achenproblem", *Neue Psychologische Studien*, No. 12,1934.

[18] *Bilingualism and Language Disabilitv*, Ed. by N. Miller, London-Sidney, 1984.

[19] K. C. Gardner, *Social Ps1Jcholoy and Second Language Learning; the Role of Atti tudes and Motivation*, London, 1985.

[20] N. V. Imedadze, *E:J:perixtal Psychologycal Studies in the Mastering and Command of a Second Language*, Tbilisi, 1979 (in Russian).

[21] J. Ronjat, *Le Developpement du Language Observe chez un Enfant Bilingue*, Paris, 1913.

[22] D. Slobin, "Cognitive prerequisites for the development of grammar", *Studies of Child Language Development*, Ed. by Ch. Ferguson and D. N. Slobin, New York, 1973.

[23] A. K. Zvonkin, R. M. Frumkina, "Free classification: models of behaviour", *Nauchno-tekhnicheskaya informatsiya,* Series 2, No. 6,1980.

[24] R. M. Frumkina, *Colour, Meaning, Similaritv,* Moscow, 1984 (in Russian).

[25] A. Zvonkin, "Small children and mathematics that are not like mathematics at all", Znaniye-sila, No. 8,1985.

SUBJECT INDEX